# NEXT LEVEL SELLING

## The Definitive Guide to Closing High Dollar Deals

## Tom Fedro

Leaders
Press

ISBN 978-1-943386-52-9 (pbk)
ISBN 978-1-943386-51-2 (ebook)
ISBN 978-1-943386-53-6 (hardcover)

Library of Congress Control Number: 2019908607

# Praise for *Next Level Selling*

This book is different from others in the way it establishes a brilliant and easy-to-follow method to sniff out a sale (or not) and close it. If you're tired of wasting time with deals that don't close, you need this book.

– **Rocky Foroutan** | CEO, LenderHomePage.com

*Next Level Selling* is a fast, fun and educating read. Tech insiders and anyone who believes in compacting the sales process will delight in this book.

– **Greg Elliott** | President, Anderson Howard

This engaging, hands-on book is the guide you need to break into the million-dollar sales club and make it happen.

– **Kent Savage** | Co-Founder & CEO,
Icon.me and Director, Centric Brands

This is a key read for a great foundational sales approach and a straight-forward method for identifying and landing the deal.

– **Jade Runnells** | CEO, Firstimpulse

This book is an indispensable roadmap for approaching your clients, and its informative content will consistently provide reading anticipation.

– **Bob Carlson** | CEO, The Carlson Company

*Next Level Selling* is a tantalizing journey into high-level sales and the challenges and triumphs you'll encounter. Fedro's humility and unwavering honesty is a refreshing voice in an industry dominated by more 'how to' books than probably any other. This book is not only highly informative, but it also restores faith in the tenacity, resilience and humanity of today's salespeople.

– **Christopher Catranis** | Founder of Babylon Telecommunications and
bestselling author of *Disruptive Leadership*

This book enables so many others to benefit from Tom Fedro's successful sales experience and knowledge. It demystifies why he has been so consistently successful, leading a team of diverse sales professionals, and helping create multiple, exceptionally profitable businesses. He distills his approach to sales leadership into eight steps that you need to know, supported throughout the book by anecdotes and stories to bring them to life. This is a great book for CEOs, as well salespeople, looking to get to the next level in generating profitable revenue.

– **Ted Larkins** | bestselling author of *Get To Be Happy*

As a CEO tasked with helping my salespeople build healthy habits to bring in the big whales of our industry, *Next Level Selling* is the playbook I have been searching for. Not only does the book offer actionable items I can teach my sales team, but I can also refer them to read and implement the ideas themselves. The format is powerful and simple. This should be taught in all business schools.

– **Jess Hartmann** | CEO, ProMAX Systems

I've read a lot to maintain my edge in business and have a strong bias for concise books with actionable information. *Next Level Selling* presents information in sensible chapters that end with a case study and lessons learned. The stories make the lessons very memorable.

– **Brian Hoshiko** | Director of SaaS Operations, CalAmp/LoJack

Tom Fedro provides a methodology and detailed approach that can guide newer and seasoned sales professionals to close large deals and expand client relationships. His case studies provide real-life examples to achieve sales success.

– **Jayson Yardley** | CEO, AvadyneHealth

As a sales entrepreneur myself, who has been on a similar path to the author, I was skeptical of the value that I'd derive from the book. I'm happy that didn't stop me from reading — there are a lot of insights, perspectives and tactics I hadn't considered before that I hope to adapt and put to use in my own ventures.

– **David Fuess** | CEO, Catapult Systems and bestselling author of *Why They Buy*

As one who does marketing for a living, I've read my fair share of books on marketing and sales leadership and most are full of lengthy stories that fill the pages but provide very little substance (kind of like that sales person we all know who talks too much!) That's the exact opposite of what you will find in *Next Level Selling*. I found not only a unique perspective on leadership, but most importantly I found a sense of genuineness that is missing from many so-called leaders these days.

– **Beverly Lages** | President, Lages & Associates

The tips are great and reflect true wisdom. Tom explains how he discovered all the commonalities to his top sales and admits areas where he learned to do things differently. Makes for a good and enlightening read, especially the case studies.

– **Mark Nureddine** | CEO, Bull Outdoor Products and bestselling author of *Pocket Mentor*

This book covers everything you need to know about selling high-value deals. The key is to have a clearly-defined process and to follow it religiously. It is all in this book, set out in a logical and readable form. Being in the same business myself, I will use it to enhance our own processes. It will definitely also become required reading for our salespeople.

– **Tony White** | CEO and Founder, enChoice, Inc.

The biggest thing I have learned from Tom Fedro's *Next Level Selling* is when to walk away from a sale — and yes, there are times when you should do so. For example, instead of courting a client that isn't going to buy (or invest in my case), cut your losses early by using Tom's analysis and go seek a sure thing. Developing this kind of ground-level vision is sure to save a lot of time and make the playing field much more profitable.

– **Daniel P. Culler** | CEO, Avistone

I shared the book with my sales team before I even finished it! *Next Level Selling* is more streamlined than the Sandler system and it's more focused on closing big deals. It clarifies the relationship between marketing and sales well, and is perfectly timed for the next phase or our team's growth.

– **Mark Wagner** | CEO, EdTechTeam

*Next Level Selling* provides lots of great advice for anyone in the sales profession. Whether you close high-ticket deals or mid-ticket deals, you'll benefit enormously from this new sales bible.

–**Ali Razi** | Founder & CEO, Banc Certified Merchant Services

Tom Fedro explains how he closes big sales in the technology space. As one working in this space, allow me to say two things. First, it's really hard work. Second, having known Tom for a few years, I know when he sets a goal, he gets it done. As such, I'd recommend this book, especially to those working in senior management and sales and marketing roles in small to medium technology companies.

– **Martyn Fricker** | General Manager, Emida International

*Next Level Selling* is a very practical handbook for individuals and sales teams, establishing meaningful concepts that help you to stay focused on what can make the difference for selling and achieve success. It explains with real examples the basics of these ideas, giving you a clearer picture of what you have ahead and help you make an easy to follow roadmap for sales.

– **Hugo Teixeira** | CEO, Farmodiética USA

This special book will change how you approach any sales opportunity you encounter. There are so many sales books out there, but this book gives you real-life insight into a practical approach of making a deal. There is no hard selling here; it completely aligns your offering with your customers' needs.

– **Greg Albertyn** | President, Pacific Power Reps

As a senior-level IT-professional for the past 30 years, I've come across more salespeople than most software engineers typically do. Time and again, I witnessed first-hand what separated the best salesperson from the rest which directly resulted in the success of the company. Tom Fedro's book captures that very essence of a successful salesperson, one that sees and seizes the opportunity.

– **Peter Matuchniak** | CTO, Maxxess Systems Inc.

*Next Level Selling* is a great book for anyone who is frustrated with their current sales process and close rates. Fedro offers some excellent tips and real world case studies to help any organization improve their win column.

— **Shane Belovsky** | COO, Emida Technologies

The main takeaway for me from *Next Level Selling* is the no-nonsense, real-world examples that Tom Fedro uses to illustrate his easy and quick assessment, **PAM** (**Pain**, **Authority** and **Money**) — if you don't have it, there's no sale. It doesn't get any simpler than that, and without it, you will never close million-dollar transactions!

— **Ken Schmitt** | Founder & CEO, TurningPoint Executive Search

I highly recommend reading this book, but more importantly, following Tom's process to analyze the viability of any sale — which is an acronym he cleverly calls **PAM**.

— **Paula Johns** | CEO, Paula Johns Communications

*Next Level Selling* is a superior road-map of how **PAM** will escort you to the highest economic levels by helping you find the **Pain**, **Authority** and **Money** to win the high-end transactions. Selling multi-million dollar deals isn't easy; however, Tom shows you how to accomplish it with logic, respect, integrity and **authority**.

— **Jack Finnell** | CEO, Growth Accelerators and author of *Do You Want to Be a Leader or a Manager?*

Fedro makes it clear that if you can't find **pain**, **authority** and **money** in a potential customer, then hit the road. Fedro makes a compelling argument that in the case of sales, you shouldn't be wasting anyone's time — yours or the client.

— **Dennis Andrews** | Divisional President, Xerox

This is a practical book and a valuable resource, highly recommended for those ready to accelerate their performance!

— **Tom Prosia** | Founder & President, BeMarketDo

In *Next Level Selling*, Fedro will show you how to change your tactics to encourage success in high value deals, and make time for new (and better) habits. *Excellent, and well worth the read.*

- **Tim Marshall** | President, Neudesic Services

For Dad —
loving father, husband and son,
extraordinary USAF fighter pilot,
architect and teacher;
a true example of what a man should be

# FREE SUPPLEMENT!

Are you searching for the key to staying healthy and setting yourself up for success?

You need to take your MEDS! I created my own personal system that helps me achieve peak performance on a daily basis and I want to share it with you.

## TAKE YOUR
## MEDS

### *MORNING ROUTINE*
### *EXERCISE · DIET · SLEEP*

## TOM FEDRO

Go to www.tomfedro.com and download your free copy of Take Your MEDS to see how you can apply and benefit from some of the same ideas that have worked so well for me.

# CONTENTS

# INTRODUCTION

**The secret of getting ahead is getting started.**
– attributed to Mark Twain

Who the heck wants to read another book on sales and marketing?

That's a fair question. If you're anything like me, you already have some seriously packed bookshelves lined with all those *other* books. You know the kind; those books that promised to teach you how to sell to the Moby Dick in your particular industry. So why would I write another book on sales and marketing when so many already glut the market?

Because I'm going to introduce you to my secret weapon — a brilliant gal I know named **PAM**. When you meet her, you'll see why the method described in the following pages has been my key to selling more than 200 million software licenses worldwide, and closing deals with many of the world's largest, most respected companies and brands — all of which led to generating hundreds of millions of dollars in sales revenue.

## What can you expect in these pages that you can't find anywhere else?

I'm going to toss over the keys for small technology companies to win big, million-dollar-plus transactions in a predictable way by building the right approach and infrastructure. You won't find all the jargon and superfluous speeches here, but you will find the tools necessary to be successful in the complex multilevel sales processes required for large deals. Step by step, you'll learn all about my proven method — one that happens to be quite easy to understand and replicate in your field.

1

Your new friend **PAM** is going to teach you precisely how to find the **pain**, establish the **authority** and confirm the **money** before you approach a single sale. **PAM** is the key to every deal and if you don't have all three of her crucial elements in a potential sale, she will tell you not to waste your time or anyone else's. You'll learn each step in the **PAM** framework, and read some compelling examples of how each step in the process works. Even a small company can effectively compete with the big dogs by establishing the kind of working sales methodology I'm going to lay out for you.

Marketing and business development can be some of the priciest parts of running a business, and in these pages, you'll learn how to trim the fat and get the most for your **money** in these strategic areas. You'll learn how to build an ideal customer profile (ICP), and discover how to teach your salespeople to close deals using a variety of tactics, including the "Domino Effect." I'm going to show you how to leverage just one domino to open new and more accessible markets for your services. As you know, salespeople aren't all the same, so you'll learn my recommended mix for the different types of salespeople to hire — and you'll meet the Maverick.

Of course, we'll also discuss the significant obstacles and mistakes you're going to make (just as I did). I'll fill you in on some of the more common ones, and share my hard-won experience earned by taking down some hairy beasts and turning them into big wins. Lastly, I'll share how to keep up with the competition by using the new toolbox we're building together.

### **Make a customer, not a sale.** – Katherine Barchetti

So, who am I and why should you listen to me? I'm just a guy fortunate to have done this many times before — so often that I have discerned a clear process that I can articulate and share with you. My job has always been to 'bring in the big one'. My career arc spans the corporate gamut. First, I served as a bag-carrying salesperson, before moving up the ranks into a VP Sales and Marketing position, and finally, landing the president and CEO role. My perspective and personal experience encompass the entire scope of the sales, marketing and executive management ecosystem.

I'm not going to share theories or 50,000-foot-level tips and tricks. Instead, we're in the trenches here and this is hand-to-hand combat; you're in a knife fight as the little guy going up against the biggest, most resourceful competitors on the planet. Let's look at an example — a deal I did with American Airlines, one of the world's largest airlines — which was no small feat. We had the kind of competition that would make an Inuit shiver, as we were just a small company of less than one hundredth of the size of our rivals. (I'm sure you're familiar with a few of their names — Acer, ASUS, Dell, IBM and Toshiba.) Reeling in this airline's mobile workforce project was the deal of the century at the time, and everyone in the business knew it, so all the major players were hunting down this transaction; big company representatives seemed to be parachuting into the parking lot daily.

At my company, GRiD Systems, we were a small brand with a small footprint, but a mighty heart, so we took off in pursuit of **PAM** and treated the airline deal the same as any other.

- First, we went in and confirmed the **pain**. Why did the prospect need this technology purchase for their mobile teams? How much did it hurt not to have new systems in place?
- Secondly, we discovered the **authority** (who was going to make the decision). We learned that the decision came down to the technical influencers who were evaluating these devices.
- Third, even though this was a multi-billion dollar company, we dug deep to confirm that the budget (**money**) for the project was in place and ready to be spent on the right partner.

## All things being equal, people will do business with and refer business to those people they know, like, and trust. – Bob Burg

My task for this deal was to work with our potential client's people and get to know them personally at a deep level. I'm sure you are aware that sales is a people business, and especially for significant purchases, we tend to buy from people we like. I had to understand their **pain**, discover exactly what they were looking for, and uncover their personal goals and desires. Beyond talking with the senior executives involved, I spent time with the top system evaluators. I learned how they wanted to move up within the ranks of the company and what it would take. I spent my time building relationships with those key influencers and then took those relationships to a more personal level.

For example, we spent time together visiting my company headquarters. I played basketball with a few of the guys. I took them out on the golf course to get to know them and discover what was going on behind the scenes, and that helped me understand the political landscape that was in play. What ultimately won the deal was getting the chief IT evaluator out on the links in Monterrey, California, as that allowed us to spend quality time in a relaxed environment. The scene was set for me to let him know I fully understood how risky it was for him to choose to go with us, and also to convince him that the rewards were significant enough to make that decision in our favor. He did, and we won the deal, which was well in excess of seven figures to start.

After getting in with the company through that first product offering, my ticket got punched into a management role where I was able to leverage our new relationships at the airline to land new projects. Over time, our team convinced them to move to our desktop products for their airport installations around the world; this achievement was accomplished to the tune of more than $20 million. We were the smallest brand in the field, yet we won this major client in front of all the major players. We turned a high-pressure situation into a win, moving the initial deal from a $2 million purchase to well in excess of $20 million in revenue while developing a much deeper, long-term relationship with the airline.

Our win there demonstrates one of the major concepts I'm going to talk about, which is that in most cases you have to get out of the office to make these deals happen. You have to relate to the prospect with a personal, one-on-one approach. In this case, the deal was high profile with many people watching. We had to meet some demanding technical requirements, and that required a lot of face time with the technical team.

**It is not your clients' and prospects' job to remember you. It is your obligation and responsibility to make sure they don't forget you.** – Patricia Fripp

I'll be the first to tell you that today's customers can be tough to reach, and that's another reason I wrote this book. The breadth of my experience spans many years touching on more than one generation, so I've had to learn in the trenches to alter my tactics and develop new ways to reach prospects. We're no longer dealing with the Me Generation; today's contemporary customer of the Digital Age has become the "i" Generation:

- isolated;
- informed;
- influenced.

What does that mean for today's small software and technology companies selling high-value software? Moreover, what if you're one of those companies that doesn't have the marketing budgets and resources seemingly needed to make the big plays to win those sales worth half a million to one million dollars (or more)?

Before Google, it was much easier to access people and get in front of them early in the sales process. They didn't have access to nearly as much data as they have now, so you'd be able to talk to them much earlier in the cycle. You could influence your standing in their eyes, and if you were in there first and fast, you could show them the value points, and close the deal before the competition even knew you were there.

It's a different game today. You're not necessarily going to have that opportunity to beat your rivals to a first meeting. Your customers will already know you and other companies with a similar offering. Sometimes your competitors are going to get in there first, and that means you're going to have to fight for mindshare.

**Your competition is everything else your prospect could conceivably spend their money on.**
– Don Cooper

You must be positioned as a consultant offering value to your potential customer's business, not just looking to sell them your particular product. You must have industry knowledge and know-how to share with them that they can use beyond your product. With so much information, though, being lobbed over the wall at today's prospect, how do you ensure you can grab that jaded and overstimulated prospect's attention?

Today, prospects stay in the information-gathering stage longer because they enjoy the freedom of information granted by the Internet; they can research more easily and access information sources that were once hidden or unavailable. Now, your prospects are able to gather details on your products, then slice and dice that research to figure out exactly what questions they have before they ever engage in the sales process. It may seem like a more efficient process now, but you need to be able to step in exactly where the customer needs you.

Executing a successful process comes down to the skills of your salespeople, as well as that of your marketing team in creating a relevant website and social media presence that drive engagement. Your salesperson needs to know whether to go in with a sniper or a blast mentality. It's critical for the salesperson to understand the people they're targeting with their message so they can go in armed with the information that grabs the prospect's attention.

## The only limit to our realization of tomorrow will be our doubts of today. – Franklin D. Roosevelt

It's entirely possible to win those big sales despite having a budget that is either small or almost non-existent. I see it all the time. Small companies with limited resources and budgets can and do make those big plays. But how do they do it?

They undoubtedly have a few things working for them, such as

- a quality, well-trained team;
- a dynamic website that educates via new information;
- key marketing and sales techniques.

Does that sound easy to achieve? It can be! I've got a process. Not only have I done it before, but I've worked with many small companies and helped them navigate their way to success as well. You're going to pick up some powerful new tips, so keep reading. It's time to unpack these ideas and discuss them in greater detail.

Let's go!

# CHAPTER 1

............................................................

# MEET PAM

**We cannot solve our problems with the same thinking we used when we created them.**
– attributed to Albert Einstein

Every deal — without exception — revolves around one conceptual package, a core set of qualities that I've previously referred to as **PAM**. While she can be elusive, she *must* be at the table for a successful sale to take place. The three components of **PAM** are **pain**, **authority** and **money**. If you can't find her when you're looking at a deal, you're probably wasting everybody's time.

For example, consider the importance of those three pieces and how crucial it is that they all work together.

- If there's no **pain**, there's no motivation to close — and no deal.
- If you have **pain**, but the person across the desk doesn't have the **authority** to make a decision — there's no deal.
- If you've found the **pain** and **authority**, but the prospect doesn't have the **money** to move forward — you don't have a deal.

I first met **PAM** in the 1990s/early 2000s when my team and I were selling large software deals in the million-dollar range (and higher). As we gained experience in our industry, various patterns came to light on the projects we won and the projects we lost. It became clear that the opportunities that we weren't closing shared common denominators. Upon closer examination, we saw that we were always missing at least one element of **PAM**.

- We didn't have solid confirmation on the **pain**.
- The cash or budget (**money**) wasn't there to move forward.
- We weren't talking to the real decision makers (**authority**).
- There was no urgency; inertia stalled progress.
- There was a failure to disclose critical details or perhaps dishonesty around **pain**, **authority** and **money**.

### Once we became aware of the patterns, we realized that closing a deal *always* required the presence of pain, authority and money.

When we analyzed each deal that we'd lost, one or more of those elements was missing, or else the prospective client had misled us or perhaps even lied to us — that unfortunately happens regularly. Some people aren't comfortable telling you the truth and will lie to avoid conflict or letting you down. (While it would be much better if they were comfortable enough to admit they would not be moving forward, sometimes that doesn't happen.)

Meeting **PAM** is the primary objective whenever you visit an account. There's no better business partner than **PAM**, I promise you. She demands and deserves a great deal of respect because she's always right. Locate her in every deal, make her your best friend, and you'll win more business than ever before. **Pain** plus **authority** plus **money** equals your deal; you have to have all three. Like death and taxes, there's no getting around that equation.

## YOUR OFFERING MUST!

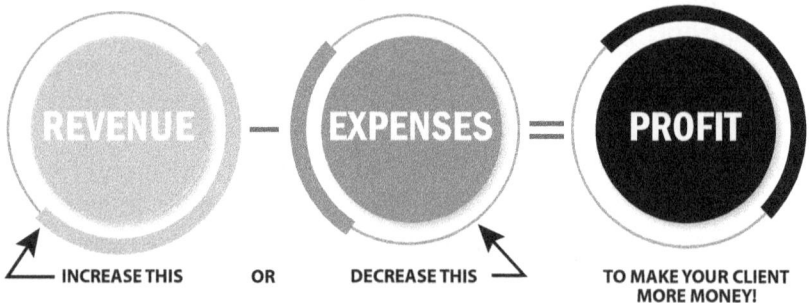

( REVENUE ) — ( EXPENSES ) = ( PROFIT )

INCREASE THIS    OR    DECREASE THIS    TO MAKE YOUR CLIENT MORE MONEY!

**PAM**'s business-minded. She only cares about one thing, and it's the one equation essential to closing high-dollar agreements. **PAM** likes three letters — REP (revenue - expenses = profit). Your solution or product — whatever you're selling — has to increase revenue or decrease expenses, and hopefully both, ultimately helping your client generate measurably more profit.

I caution you that inviting **PAM** to the table isn't a one-shot deal. Make sure that **PAM** is fully understood, confirmed, and reconfirmed throughout the sales process. Change can occur and often will as you're working with a prospect; people come and go, or perhaps a new CEO comes on board while you're working a sale. Be sure that for the length of the selling journey, **PAM** is right by your side, signaling imminent success.

### →Finding the pain↓

# A person's success in life can be measured by the number of uncomfortable conversations he or she is willing to have. – Tim Ferriss

When it comes to large, million-dollar-plus software and technology transactions in the business world, **pain** is beyond the 'nice to have' category; it's required for a successful sale. The kind of **pain PAM** requires needs to be solved and it needed to happen yesterday. When you and your prospective client have identified why they're either losing **money** or missing out on making more, you're creating a well-defined path edged with urgency that steers them toward your solution.

Hone the quality of your discovery questions to understand the depth of that **pain**. Identify it, codify it, and put it down on paper so everybody sees how big the **pain** is. Peel back the onion to determine the source of the **pain**. Examine what your prospect has done in the past, and why it didn't work. Ask a whole series of questions to understand what's causing the **pain**, the consequent bleeding of cash in some cases or the inability to take advantage of a market opportunity. Show the prospect how your product or service can solve their **pain** points.

This process might at first feel frustrating; a pull-your-hair-out part of the process that slows progress. Feel confident, though, that once you've uncovered **pain** of that magnitude, you'll be sitting in the catbird seat. The number of eyeballs on the issue once you draw their attention to that **pain** will multiply. When you show that your product or service offering is going to ease that **pain** across their organization, you've significantly improved your chances of winning the business.

Remember, however, that closing the sale will invariably come down to the REP: R minus E equals P — increase revenue or decrease expenses to increase profits. Explain which part of that equation your product or service will address for your prospect.

### →Finding the authority↓

## Sales are contingent upon the attitude of the salesman, not the attitude of the prospect.
### – William Clement Stone

Finding the **authority** in your prospect's organization could very well involve guessing to a certain extent, based on your understanding of the vertical market and the prospect's particular spot in the ecosystem. You could guess based on an organizational chart or prior deals but ideally, your marketing department has worked closely with sales to define the ideal customer profile (See Chapter 2.) and pulled together an updated and appropriate contact database.

Be sure to do your research on those contacts once you've identified them. Review their profiles. You need to know that, for example, the CIO is going to be the ultimate decision maker, while his director of security software and his technical team are going to be the key influencers in selecting which offering to accept. Once you've identified the critical roles, make contact, and set the meeting to determine if there's **pain**. Get in there and ask your discovery questions until you clearly understand who in the organization has the **authority** to decide in favor of your offering.

### →Finding the money↓

## The same wind blows on us all... It is not the blowing of the wind, but the setting of the sails that will determine our direction... – Jim Rohn

With this step, as with the others, it's the salesperson's job to do sufficient research before deploying significant resources in a pre-sales environment. You must ensure the cash is there. You must also understand that although the prospect has the **money** to move forward with your solution, you may not yet understand their particular situation affecting their financial decisions.

Make sure they understand how the **money** spent with you will improve their business. Establish the value you're providing, the **pain** you're eliminating and the great feeling that you're going to provide for those stakeholders once the deal is completed. Once you've made it through the first two gauntlets, you have certainly earned the right to confirm that the cash is budgeted and ready to be spent on your project, and that empowers pre-sales resources to organize for the next step in the process.

During the discovery process, you will have already identified the **pain** and the associated cost with the prospects you approach, so the price shouldn't be a scary discussion at that point. Instead, it's a brilliant opportunity to review with your prospect how much **money** they're going to save over time by using your product.

### Don't sell life insurance. Sell what life insurance can do. – Ben Feldman

## Case study: Rogers Communications
### *The Hail Mary*

Rogers Communications is a Toronto-based innovator in communications services that offers wireless services to more than 10.1 million subscribers, along with cable television, telephone, Internet and home monitoring. They also provide business communications services, and strive to bring world-class innovations to their customers.

The company's **pain** was their need for a software platform to monitor their wireless network for fraudulent users. The company was losing revenue and wasting their airtime on illegal, fraudulent subscribers. Those fraudsters would use sophisticated equipment to capture a phone number right out of the air and put it into another device for use on the network — a cloned phone. They got away with free usage, wasting valuable airtime, while the customer got hit with the bill.

The level of fraudulent activity soon became a nightmare for everybody involved, including customer service, the consumer and the revenue assurance team responsible for making sure the cash was collected. This was real **pain** that Rogers (as well as every major wireless network provider in the world) was facing. Rogers needed a software platform to monitor their wireless network and flag fraudulent users for immediate termination.

The **authority** to make the decision had risen to the CEO of the company, but the people making the recommendation of which vendor to choose were the technical and end-user evaluators in the revenue assurance department. They were tasked with seeing how our product (and competing offerings) would integrate with their existing systems, and how comfortable their users would be interacting with the product. The project lead and procurement confirmed the **money** to pay for the project as the **pain** had become acute. **PAM** was definitely in the building!

Unfortunately, the technical team chose a competitor's product and recommended it to senior management and the CEO instead of ours. We asked why the decision went the other way, but our many queries went unanswered after months of hard work. We were confident that our solution was the best fit, and decided to pull out all the stops and throw the Hail Mary pass.

We created a compelling communication to the CEO, pointing out our top position in the market while sharing more details on how many of his peers and competitors were using our solution. We provided deep industry insights that we had shared with the evaluation team but felt might not have made it to the executive suite. Our compelling communication was the key to reopening the opportunity and getting us back in the door for more detailed discussions (with the CEO's blessing). Ultimately, we won the business, snatching victory from the jaws of defeat!

## Lessons learned

You have to build relationships at the executive level, as well as the technical evaluation level and the mid-management level. Having senior-level visibility is what lands the big deals in many cases. It's always best to have a multilevel approach throughout the deal-making process. In this case, we should have been in the executive suite with **PAM** earlier in the process. A win is a win, however, and as Winston Churchill said, "Never, never, never give up." That Hail Mary letter was the key to great success for the team and was worth well in excess of $1 million in net new revenue for the company.

---

### The three components of **PAM** are **pain**, **authority** and **money**.

- If there's no **pain**, there's no motivation to close — and no deal.

- If you have **pain**, but the person across the desk doesn't have the **authority** to make a decision — there's no deal.

- If you've found the **pain** and **authority**, but the prospect doesn't have the **money** to move forward — you don't have a deal.

Closing a deal requires the presence of **pain**, **authority** and **money**.

---

# THE PROVEN
# PAM SALES PROCESS

**01** IDENTIFY - Identify the specific prospect within the Ideal Customer Profile (ICP) database.

**02** ENGAGE - Engage the prospect and establish a warm connection that will allow the salesperson to move into a natural and empathetic discovery process to identify and feel their PAIN. (If there is no pain, professionally disengage and move on to the next prospect.)

**03** PAIN - One the PAIN is identified, discovery continues: the PAIN must be completely broken down and understood. Why is it happening? Is it getting worse? When did it start? Ask these questions and more.

**04** AUTHORITY - Once the PAIN has been established, the AUTHORITY to make a decision must be identified and confirmed. Who will ultimately be involved in the decision to buy?

**05** MONEY - Is the budget available to solve their identified PAIN? Budget questions must be asked to ensure that a deal can be closed, provided the proposed solution eliminates the PAIN.

**06** PROPOSAL, NEGOTIATION, & CLOSURE - Deliver the promised solution that eliminates the PAIN for the prospect in a compelling and financially-acceptable way. Done properly, this leads to a natural close where discounts and trials are not necessary - sign the deal and move on to implementation.

**07** IMPLEMENTATION OF THE SOLUTION - Implementation is generally handled by a separate group, but the salesperson needs to be ready to assist their teammates should things go south — and they should stand as an advocate for the client when issues arise. This is where business relationships and future referrals are cemented.

**08** GROWTH AND RENEWAL - Good salespeople always stay in touch with their contacts who have now become paying customers — this is where new business within that organization can be identified and renewal business for years to come continues to be assured.

*PAM Needs to Be in the Building In Order to Win!*

# CHAPTER 2

# A MILLION-DOLLAR FRAMEWORK

**Prospecting — find the man with the problem.**
– Ben Friedman

There are eight critical steps to finding **PAM** and building long-term relationships — and those steps make up what we call a million-dollar framework. It's vital that you comprehend and internalize each part of this framework.

1. Identify the ideal customer profile.
2. Engage the prospect.
3. Ask quality questions to establish the **pain**.
4. Establish the **authority**.
5. Ensure the **money** is there.
6. Create a compelling proposal.
7. Implementation
8. Growth and renewal

## 1. Identify the ideal customer profile (ICP).

The ICP is a relatively well-understood concept, so let's dive straight into discussing the ICP as it relates to **PAM**. Consider the look of the ideal customer in your industry. Examine metrics, such as the size of the company by revenue and employee count, their vertical market, geographic location and which vendors they currently use. Are they growing or shrinking? Who are their competitors? Once you've roughed out a profile, you can create a database of prospects. (See Chapter 3.)

The ICP identifies prospects most likely to have **PAM** dancing in the halls of their buildings. Your ICP will describe who is most likely to invest in your product or service, and will become the guiding light for all of your marketing and sales messages. Your ICP places a laser focus on the specific prospects who will love your product, derive the most value from it, and — once they become customers — will stay with you, buy more, and become a strong advocate and referral source for you.

Correctly identifying the ICP shortens the sales cycle, as these prospects are probably already feeling the **pain** that your product will reduce or eliminate. The most qualified of these prospects are already seeking a product or service like yours and may already use one of your competitors. Your sales and marketing team will be much more effective with an identified ICP as it will put their attention on repeatable and scalable sales strategies with the right message targeting the right prospects. You can nail down a universe of potential suspects into pre-qualified prospects that fit in the box where your product or service will do the most good — helping them reach their goals and alleviating their **pain** to the benefit of all.

Established companies can identify their particular ICP by asking questions of the existing customer base. Determine their defining characteristics, and then classify the people that are currently using your product or service. Ask how they feel about it. The answers to these and other fundamental questions will give you a strong feel for your ICP.

Look at your existing customers, and identify common elements such as these.

- Who is getting the most value out of the product?
- Who is getting the best return on their investment?
- Who has stayed with you for the long haul?
- Which of these customers is providing you with the most profit?

- Who is returning your product?
- Who is calling for support?
- Who continues to buy your product?

These questions will reveal the general shape of your ICP, allowing you to drill deeper with more specific questions such as these.

- Market     What is their industry or vertical market?
- Pattern     In which SIC code are they classified?
- Size     How big are they by employee count and locations?
- Income     What's their annual revenue?
- Geography     Where are they located — domestic to the U.S. or international?
- Maturity     How old are they?
  Are they a startup or newer company?
  What kind of pattern can we find in the age of the business?
  Is it growing or shrinking?
  Are competitors moving into their market?
  Or are they being bought?
- Technology     If you are selling a software solution, you'll want to know what systems and software they have in place, and how that impacts your offering.
  Will your offering work with whatever they have in place?

  For example, if they're an ORACLE ERP shop and your product only works with SAP, you could have a problem. Do they have enough people for your offering? They may have substantial revenue, but few employees. If you're selling payroll software or HR software based on employee count, that's an important metric.

After you collect and analyze the answers to your questions, you should have a solid ICP describing the most profitable prospects to pursue with your advertising and messaging.

Let's say you've analyzed the relevant and critical demographic categories to build your ICP. You've learned the following.

- They're based in the United States.
- They bring in $300 million and above in annual revenue.
- They're in the healthcare industry.
- They've been in business for 20 years.
- They use a particular kind of clinical database (that you sell).

With that profile, you can confidently nail down a tight group of prospects. The next step for each of those prospects is to identify the key personas in your ICP.

## Opportunities don't happen; you create them.
### – Chris Grosser

## What's a persona anyway?

According to an article by Amy Wright with the title "What Is a 'Buyer Persona' and Why Is It Important?" (*Social Media Today*, October 17, 2017),

> "A buyer persona is a research-based profile that depicts a target customer. Buyer personas describe who your ideal customers are, what their days are like, the challenges they face and how they make decisions."

She adds,

> "It's common to have *multiple* buyer personas for a business — for example, if the end user of your product needs to gain the approval of others before making a purchase, each individual involved in that decision is a separate persona. They'll have different criteria for evaluating your product, and you'll need different strategies to address those needs."

The ICP should include the demographics of an account and the people you'll target, such as the influencers and decision makers; this is where defining specific buyer personas becomes critical. Add these details to the overall ICP to help you prepare. For example, if you're selling a software product, you'll want to talk to the engineers or technical people within an account. In many cases, they will be at the level of director or manager.

## What are their potential goals?

As you get deeper into defining the ICP and buyer personas, ask what it is they are looking to accomplish; what their near-term and long-term goals are; and what they feel to be the critical issues that keep coming up meeting after meeting, quarter after quarter. Find their **pain** and develop an understanding of the hot buttons for that particular group. Going through this process with your existing customers (or focus groups for startups) will define their **pain** envelope and prepare for validating it across your prospect base.

## Who is the end user?

The end user is a separate persona, who will be much more interested in how easily the product fits into their daily efforts, rather than a technical evaluator, who will be looking at how easily it fits into their existing environment. Will the product increase or decrease the amount of time they're sitting behind a computer? Which benefits and messages will resonate with the end user?

## What is the message for the authority?

Generally, the financial buyer in high-value, million-dollar-plus transactions will be the CFO, a vice-president of finance and in some cases, a director — the individual who will be evaluating the nuts and bolts on the return on investment. Although they release the funds, Finance is NOT the ultimate decision maker in most cases — so who is? Who inks the deal? Whether that's an individual manager, director, VP, the CEO or a group of nameless faces that are on the committee, you must determine the best message for the **authority**. The titles may vary for each prospect even though they are grouped in your ICP database.

After running through this maze, you'll have mapped out the account. You'll know the ICP, the demographics, the four or five persons involved in the sale, and you will have developed particular messages for each one of them.

Now get out there and make it happen!

## 2. Engage the prospect.

There are multiple ways to initiate outbound engagement, but the most direct and effective vector is email (ideally that they've opted in to receive), followed by phone, then text message, then FedEx and then direct mail — with the shared goal of every outreach being to entice the prospect to meet, in person if appropriate. Use LinkedIn's platform to engage the prospect, hammer social media where your buyer personas spend their time, and start a webinar series to deliver valuable content. Be visible at industry trade shows where you're building your brand in front of the right crowd, many of them fitting your ICP. Do what you can to find out what your particular prospects will respond to and leverage that insight.

Email has proven to be the most effective method for reaching out to large groups with targeted communications. A tight message will get the best response. That, however, is your 'air cover' to provide great overall coverage. Be aware that you'll be dealing with many spam traps and anti-spam rules that might prevent your email from reaching your target, so makes sure you're getting people to opt in to your mailing list via your website, and find other ways to engage as well.

When you're dealing with million-dollar deals, you'll need to be assertive and creative in reaching your prospect. Beyond email, you must hit the phones, text messaging, follow up with a FedEx, UPS or DHL package if necessary (since it's a million-dollar deal, the extra cost is worth it — as long as you direct it to the right person's desk), followed by another voicemail and more outreach on social media. Do whatever you can to snag their attention and get in there!

## In the middle of every difficulty lies opportunity. – Albert Einstein

Figure out the right avenue to get to the prospect, whether it's through originality, repetition or passion. Perhaps you can land an introduction through your business network or a friend of a friend. You'll need to be incredibly resourceful to make it happen, but that's the job. With your ICP, it's a foregone conclusion that they'll enjoy a significant return on investment, just as your other customers have. Closing the deal also means a huge revenue win for the salesperson's company which means a big commission check for the salesperson. Win, win, win — the circle of life in business!

## What about the gatekeeper?

Many books have been written on the gatekeeper, so we won't spend much time on the subject. At this level of selling, you'll be dealing with senior-level decision makers, making it more likely that you will encounter a gatekeeper. My advice is not to play any games. Don't pull ridiculous stunts to get someone on the phone. I've been witness to some crazy stuff, including hearing someone drop a line like "Hey, your guy owes me **money**. Let me talk to him." Another tactic would be to leave a voicemail and after listing your phone number, pretend to be cut off right before telling the prospect how much they won in the lottery.

These tactics won't work. Don't do it! Once your cover's blown, they're not going to be too impressed by your level of deception, and they're going to shut you down. I recommend that you always be honest and explain precisely why you're calling. Instead of being deceitful, make the gatekeeper your advocate. Explain the value you've provided to other key players in the industry. Share that you have some insights on their competition that would be very helpful to the target. Offer to send them some of the info directly. Sell them on the value of a few minutes of their charge's time with you and your information.

In many cases, they'll put you on the calendar — if you've done an excellent job presenting yourself. If not, they may recommend you to somebody else who is the key influencer or a potential decision maker. It's always going to be much more powerful to come down to that person with a recommendation from the CEO or CTO than to call them out of the blue. The gatekeeper must be your friend, and you must do whatever you can to convince them that you're worthy of time with the target.

If that doesn't work — say the gatekeeper takes the form of a lower-level manager yet claims to be the decision maker — you can utilize multilevel selling. For example, say you're speaking to an IT director, and you need to reach the vice president, who is the **authority**. Request an appointment by saying, "I'd like to bring my vice president to meet with you and your vice president to review our understanding. We can give you a briefing on the industry from our perspective, and provide competitive information that we feel you would find highly valuable. Can we set up a meeting?" You can secure the audience you need by using someone within your organization to do a multilevel sales call.

This method is highly effective. If you've got some good details, it's going to make this director look good to put you in front of their VP because the company's going to get some inside information that otherwise they'll never have. It's a powerful tactic to use with everybody up and down the executive suite in your company to close deals.

## Every sale has five obstacles: no need, no money, no hurry, no desire, no trust. – Zig Ziglar

## How do you establish your credibility and show that you're somebody to be taken seriously?

If you have good reference accounts, it always helps to talk about the other people who are successfully using your solution. If you're a new company and you don't have many customers in your particular market, how do you establish your credibility? Create the opportunity for that first prospect to become an excellent reference account! Do whatever is necessary to close with them — you could give them special treatment such as free engineering resources, extended maintenance or new features that can be leveraged by future customers and delivered at no charge. Again, it's all about being creative in pursuit of your goal — that's the nature of the sales business.

Remember my *Hail Mary* story from the previous chapter? To win that first big deal (or even the first deal), there has to be a clear incentive for the prospect to take a risk with a small upstart. Everyone understands that choosing a newbie would result in much more scrutiny if something goes awry. I suggest that you identify and engage an internal champion — somebody in the account who is not afraid to take chances and make a name for themselves. A champion inside can be the key (and many times the only way) to win that business.

## Most people think 'selling' is the same as 'talking'. But the most effective salespeople know that listening is the most important part of their job. – Roy Bartell

For a small company to compete, it's always helpful for them to find somebody on the inside with a mindset focused on making the right decision, regardless of anything else. The brand on the service or product they're buying doesn't matter; they don't have to buy from the biggest name in the industry. They want the right deal with the right perks, and if it's a small company that can prove themselves, they'll go ahead and choose them. Finding and leveraging this type of champion in these potential reference accounts is the fastest, most efficient path to victory.

## What if you have some reference accounts, but now you want to move into adjacent markets?

As the salesperson, it's your job early in the process to make sure you're dealing with an innovative organization as the first prospect for a new vertical. It becomes clear quite quickly if you're dealing with people who are not going to take chances. You've got to be able to go in and lay it out, saying, "We haven't been in this vertical before. We haven't been in this market before. We believe, though, that we have the right product. We have done our research and know how to solve the **pain** just as we have for our customers in market X, and we know how to deliver our value on time and under budget."

Lay out all your research, and confirm your ideas along with the benefits and perks they will receive as your first reference account. Review the go-forward plan, and if it's on target for this new prospect, ask them the fundamental questions about going with your company. If you're a new name, brand or solution provider in their space, are they willing to take on the risk together with you in a partnership? If not, it's time to move on. **PAM** is not in the building; it's time to go.

# Don't watch the clock; do what it does. Keep going.
## – Sam Levenson

To be successful with new prospects in new industries and verticals, make sure you get plenty of practice. Step out of your comfort zone and get into situations where you may feel awkward and uncomfortable, yet you're still required to perform. The more of those environments you can master as a salesperson, the faster you're going to grow, and the more skilled on your feet you're going to be. For an inexperienced person, of course, it's helpful to have a mentor or a resource that they can talk to and learn from. Get some training, onboarding and online role-playing, then go out there and be awkward — the more, the better for long-term success!

You must persevere. Believe in yourself, have confidence, and stretch your mind and social skills. I recommend practicing these types of skills in everyday interactions. For example, be nice to people and engage strangers. Talk to people at the supermarket or on the elevator. Practice making connections, and learn how to build that rapport as quickly as you can with each new person. Being a nice person and interacting with people improves your confidence, and you can take that to the sales table.

Here's a tip. Always have your trusty question list in your notebook; if things go sideways, you can get right back on track with quality questions ready to go. These are your roadmap to **PAM**.

## It ain't over 'til it's over. – Yogi Berra

When reaching out to prospects, the possibility exists that you could blow it. What if you leave a negative first impression? What if you don't click with the person you're talking to, or there's a *faux pas*? You apologize (if necessary) and try again. Sometimes, you catch people at the wrong moment or you remind them of someone they don't like. Perhaps their boss just chewed them out. Maybe they don't want to talk, and you happen to walk in or call right at that moment. That happens; people can be complicated. Try a different method of communication and get back in there. Your job as a sales professional is to get into that account and help them see their **pain** in the right light.

It's important to remember that you, as a salesperson, are there to help them become more profitable. You must have **PAM** and it must be a win-win scenario, or it's time to move on.

Sometimes, a company might want to assign a different salesperson to that sale, particularly if it becomes blatantly obvious that there's a personality conflict among those currently involved, or if some non-recoverable situation has taken place. It depends on what's gone down — but you can never give up if you know the prospect matches the ICP and shows signs of **PAM**; sometimes, you have to find another way in.

In some cases, it makes sense to go above the problem, avoid the initial contact altogether, and have a higher-level individual make contact with a peer in the prospect's business (for example, VP to VP or perhaps CEO to CEO). A multilevel approach can sometimes change the vector of the relationship for the better. If you believe that there's **pain** to be solved and you can do it, it's in everybody's best interests to get past the personality conflict and get down to business. It might be necessary to back off for six months and then come back. People move; people change. People get fired; people leave. It happens all the time. Don't ever give up if all the ingredients for a significant win are within reach.

## 3. Ask quality questions to establish the pain.

- Why is the **pain** happening?
- Is it getting worse?
- When did it start?
- Can we solve it?

During this discovery process, you learn more about the potential customer and their unique needs. Most of the time, quality discovery questions about **pain** will be open-ended to encourage the prospect to discuss their business candidly. They can help open the lines of communication and get to the heart of the current issues that are causing them either to lose **money** or miss opportunities to make **money**. Your industry expertise comes in here, allowing you to demonstrate how your offering can mitigate or eliminate their **pain** by sharing how well it's worked with your existing customers in the same space.

For example, you could ask these questions.

- What is the biggest challenge in growing your business?
- We have found that typical clients experience challenges like A, B or C. Which one of these resonates with you?
- How long has this been a problem?
- What have you done about your **pain** to date?
- Everybody has challenges they are dealing with. What are yours?
- What would make your work life easier and more productive?
- What challenges or current blunders are costing you the most **money**?
- Is there anything that you find to be continually wasting your time? What is it?
- Which process or activity needs to be changed or improved?
- What would you say are management's top priorities this quarter and this year?
- What's standing in the way of you achieving your priorities?
- What would increase the likelihood of switching your business to my company?
- What could hold you back from making a decision this quarter?
- What should I be asking that I haven't?

(Note that none of these questions can be answered with "Yes" or "No".)

After each question, always, always, always — without exception — say, "Tell me more about that." Keep pulling on the thread until you've unraveled the entire sweater. It's critical to a successful sales engagement that your prospect is talking 80 percent of the time because that's the only way to sell. You have to understand where they stand and allow them to explain their issues to you so that you can respond with the right solution. If you're talking about your product or your feature set, you're not selling; you're telling. In million-dollar deals, that's a sure sign of an amateur, and the customer can smell it.

## Sell, don't tell!

After this process, if all parties are in agreement that the prospect has measurable **pain**, it's much easier to start the process of positioning yourself, your company and your solution as the most effective way to eliminate that **pain** in the shortest possible time frame.

Invariably, you will find that many people don't want to talk about **pain**; they'd rather forget about it and hope it goes away. It's something they're dealing with, and they know they have to deal with it, but there can be a lot of anxiety around the discussion, and that's understandable. They have to make a decision, and it might mean spending a million bucks. Some people feel it would be better to analyze the problem a little bit longer and put it off till next year — or until they get a promotion, get the heck out of the division, and pass the buck to the next guy.

You have no choice but to wade through those invisible currents. Pull on your waders and work with your prospect to get everything out on the table so that you have a clear look at where they really stand. Learn the hazards to avoid and where to move to reach the next step in the sales process. Perhaps you could ask here what's holding them back from making a decision that quarter. Is there anything you should be asking that you haven't?

When you engage in the line of questioning I listed above, many times people will open up about their real issues — as many things that affect a business decision can be personal. Maybe the prospect is getting ready to retire, or they're expecting a new baby, and they don't want to rock the boat right now. As a salesperson, your job is to get to the real reason why a decision is not happening. You must discover all the obstacles that are impeding progress on signing a deal. The quality of your questions will determine your success in million-dollar opportunities.

### Everything you've ever wanted is on the other side of fear. – George Addair

If you confirmed the **pain** early in your set of questions, you should continue asking more questions to ensure you fully grasp the depth of the **pain** and verify that it is felt throughout the business. Is the perception of the **pain** evident to others beside your particular contact? Be sure to confirm the **pain** with multiple representatives in each affected department, and get everyone talking and educated on the **pain**.

The more people are talking, the more you're going to learn, so dig as deep as you can. How long has the **pain** been there? How much **money** have they spent trying to fix it in the past? Why is it still here? Once you've identified and quantified the **pain**, you can map that to numbers showing how much it's costing the company versus what their investment in your solution would be. Things are getting interesting.

## Change before you have to. – Jack Welch

## Know when to adjust your discovery tactics.

Develop the ability to differentiate between selling to lower levels and C-level individuals. Why? Because the higher up the food chain these authorities are, the more likely it is that they will be afflicted with discovery fatigue. When you're talking to C-Suite executives, they don't want to answer elementary discovery questions such as "What's keeping you up at night?" and "What are your objectives?"

These executives want and expect you to already understand that information due to your excellent research and/or previous interaction with their subordinates. What they want to talk about is what *should* be keeping them up at night. They want new information; they want to hear about threats they haven't already foreseen.

When you're in front of these types of decision makers, refine your tactics. Instead of asking 12 questions, drill it down to three or four. Spend the rest of your time sharing critical industry information that they may not know. Share with them what their competitors are doing that could be of significant value. Become a trusted source and advisor to senior-level executives in your targets, as it builds trust up and down the line — that's how you're going to earn your **money** when you've made it to the C-Suites.

## 4. Establish the authority.

Once the **pain** is confirmed, identify the power to authorize the purchase. Who can say "Yes," and ink the deal? **Authority** could be one person, a few people or a group, depending on the particular account and the situation. What research should you do beforehand to ensure you're connecting with the correct individual?

I suggest that this is where you utilize the best tools you can get your hands on. If you have a subscription to one of the database services, such as DiscoverOrg, Hoovers, InsideView and ZoomInfo, you already know they're great resources to map out an account by learning titles and where people fit in the organization. There is also free information on LinkedIn or if they're a public company, you can read annual shareholder reports to confirm where your target is.

Generally, you're going to have an idea of where to find the **authority** based on title, history and your ICP database. If you're an established company, you'll know how deals concluded in the past, who made those calls and who signed off on the deals. If you're a startup, you're going to do some guesswork, but you should understand most agreements are going to flow through the financial people at the end of the day. You should know who they are, but they won't always be the final word on the deal. What your solution does and who the end user is will help determine which departments (and who in those departments) are likely to be involved in the final decision to invest in your offering, and have the **authority** to sign the deal.

## Fortune favors the bold.

It's always helpful to gather information about the account from the inside before you make your first contact or run at the actual sales process. If you're trying to get into Google, you may want to establish relationships with some Googlers even though they might not be in your circles. For example, leverage friends of friends in your LinkedIn network; find out where your connections are connected with people who work for Google, and set up an exploratory lunch. You could say, "Bill's a great friend of mine, and I see you too are connected with him. He suggested I reach out due to your extensive experience with Google. They're a potential prospect of mine and your time with them is very interesting to me. I'd love to take you to lunch to learn your thoughts, and we can make fun of Bill too!"

Use lunch to learn about that account. The more information you can gather before you go deep into your sales campaign, the better off you'll be. You could discover someone on the inside who has influence, helping your initial contact get to the right person. I should say that in my career, I haven't often seen a casual relationship like this get you to the right level. It's rare that it does, though it can happen. The value of these contacts is in gaining more inside information concerning what the priorities and issues are, and perhaps learning top management's two or three critical objectives for the next three years. You could gather information like that from anybody in the company, and it will always be helpful as you prepare your pitch.

LinkedIn can be a beneficial resource. Any information you can gain about an account or an individual within an account you're targeting is going to be useful, of course. Use LinkedIn to help map out important contacts and document useful information about their personality, likes and dislikes, education history and even their interests and hobbies (such as what kind of art they like or which sports they enjoy). With LinkedIn Premium, you can even find more data, such as the contact's company growth trends, recent hires, notable alumni (perhaps finding people you already know) and executives who have recently left. Those details let you start the relationship, knowing what you might have in common. It's still true that people buy from people they like, and the more you have in common with someone, the more likely you'll be to form a productive relationship.

Additionally, working through your network to find people who have relationships with that account can be helpful. Look for non-competing vendors that have already been successful with that account. For example, if you're selling security software, you may be able to find out who sold them their ERP software or their backup solution. Find the rep and see if you can take them to lunch or collaborate on the phone and pick their brain. See who had the final **authority** on their deal, learn about the process, and ask how long it took to close. Perhaps they'll share details on the prospect's political landscape, such as who and what can kill a deal, or drop the names of some key people you don't already know. Collecting as much information as possible beforehand gives you a much better picture of what it will take to win.

**The key to mastering any kind of sales is switching statements about you — how great you are, and what you do — to statements about them.**
– Jeffrey Gitomer

Once you're in the account and the **pain** is established, it's appropriate to ask questions such as who else would be involved in signing off on the decision and how the decision process would flow for the investment. Be candid in mapping out how the deal will happen because you know you've got the goods, and you know they're going to want them.

If you find that you're speaking to someone lacking **authority**, gracefully ask to talk to someone else. This can get touchy. People like to be in control, and they want to accomplish as much as they can before bringing their boss in. You've got to respect the process; however, the Director, VP or the CEO — whoever is going to be the ultimate decision maker — has to be identified. You may not have to meet with that person to win the sale, but it's imperative to identify who ultimately has the final say. If things go south, you can then always go back to the top for another bite at the apple (as you saw in my *Hail Mary* case study).

If you find yourself at a mid-manager roadblock in large deals where seven-figure investment decisions are being made, try working the multilevel selling approach previously discussed. Offering to bring in a senior-level executive from your own team may be the only way to move up the chain on their team.

## No one can make you feel inferior without your consent. – Eleanor Roosevelt

For example, you could say, "I'd like to bring in our vice president of customer support to meet with your technical vice president so that we can be on the same page when we're putting our proposal together for support requirements." That's not intimidating to the manager, but it's going to get you in front of that decision maker who needs to hear your unfiltered story and pitch. Multilevel selling is a smart and proven sales tactic that can bring in new pairs of eyes on both sides to help push your proposal on to the next step in the sales process.

Many times, you will have a situation where a C-level executive refuses the meeting, and you'll be directed to their subordinates as appropriate. Of course, you'll run into this because their job is not to get involved; they've got a lot on their plate. Unless and until it becomes clear that the C-level executive's top priority is the elimination of the **pain** that your solution addresses, you're not going to be able to get to that ultimate decision maker; they will be relying on their team's recommendation. In this case, it's going to have to be dealt with at the appropriate level that the **pain** rises to, and your job is to make sure you know where that is and who's driving the bus into the decision maker's office with the final recommendation.

Say your prospect has a significant data breach discussed on ABC News, then your security software has a much better chance of getting you into the CEO's office in a much more timely fashion at that point. Exploit what's happening in the world, particularly as it relates to your prospect; in our selling security solutions example, use that general anxiety around data breaches to create a sense of urgency. If, however, there haven't been any notable breaches or problems lately, well, everybody knows that it's great to have good security, but it might not be a high priority. The process to decide on investment is likely to happen at a lower level. Your job is to get in front of those who can recommend your solution to the people who will spend the **money**. Give them the information and resources they need to show return on investment and why it makes perfect sense to close the deal.

In those cases, you may never actually meet that final **authority**. Your argument must be compelling enough that the people who have evaluated your offering and are going to use your product are convinced, and can clearly articulate the ROI and benefits associated with a 'go' decision for your offering to the powers that be. Build enough trust in your contacts that they are comfortable putting their reputations on the line.

### Our greatest weakness lies in giving up. The most certain way to succeed is always to try just one more time. – Thomas Edison

To get to this juncture (using our selling security solutions example), it's critical to bring the industry knowledge and competitive information that you've gathered as a sales professional to the table in a way that makes sense and is recognized as valuable. Perhaps they haven't seen, understood, or synthesized multiple events around the world that could potentially impact their business. Create a sense of urgency around the idea that these massive customer data breaches are real and are moving in on retail in a much more insidious way than they might realize.

Explain that these breaches are evolving from the billion-dollar behemoths, such as Equifax, Marriott and Target, down to the mid-enterprise companies of less than $500 million. If your prospect doesn't have the right mix of services in place to protect their network, they could fall victim to those same attacks. Drive down into specifics that aren't splashed all over the news; find the value you can bring that isn't already known and publicized. That's where the industry expertise, knowledge and anecdotes can shoot you up to the next level, or get your internal champion up to that level in financial meetings so they can get the cash for your solution appropriated.

## Winning isn't everything, but wanting to win is. – Vince Lombardi

## 5. Ensure the money is there.

Acknowledge that you have found the **pain** and **authority**, then ensure that the **money** for the purchase is there.

In some cases, the same person who has the **authority** can confirm the **money**, but it may be a budgeted opportunity. You have to get inside the account and understand their particular situation (including their needs, goals and financials) because it can be significantly different from what you perceive on social media. You have to be inside the business to do that kind of research.

In a public company, you can always look at annual reports and see their financials. Where a company may be highly profitable, they might've missed their growth numbers by 2 percent, so they're not going to spend any **money** at that time. Another company might be losing **money**, millions and millions of dollars in the red, yet they're ready to spend a ton of cash because your solution could help them close the spigot. It's the salesperson's job to get in and confirm the **money** is ready to be invested.

I suggest you ask straight up, "Assuming that our solution eliminates the **pain** and provides a return on investment that's greater than the finance requires, is the **money** budgeted and available so we can wrap this up by the end of the quarter?" A question like that is quite straightforward, and they have to be able to answer "Yes" or "No". If they can't answer it, you've got a little red flag there prompting you to pull that thread a little more to see where the **money** falls out.

## Today is always the most productive day of your week. – Mark Hunter

If the outright question doesn't fit the scenario, there are some conversational gambits you can use to feel out the prospective client's budget without being so direct. You're in the business to solve problems and eliminate the **pain** for the client, so you need to spend your resources frugally. If they don't have the **money** to invest, you must move on to the next prospect. Don't burn any bridges. You can deliver value with information provided to a prospect, and be welcomed back when the **money** becomes available. You have to understand where things stand to make the right business decision for a given potential sale.

At our company, we more or less tend to go straight for the prize. We ask if there is any **money** currently budgeted or earmarked for their project. If it's a "No", we say that we understand and we talk a little bit about why we're so successful elsewhere. We show what a company just like theirs has done and how we were able to save them **money**, demonstrating why they invested in us and have been a customer of ours for multiple years.

You have to be open so that the prospect can understand why other people are spending **money** on **pain** like theirs. Ask why they don't have it budgeted. Try to get a crack in the case where they'll offer to take another look; they probably do need what you're selling or you wouldn't be there in the first place. If not, you've done the job. No **PAM**; it's time to move on.

You got in there. You met people. You showed them how other people are using your product and how you eliminated and mitigated their **pain**, providing measurable savings and a quantifiable return on investment. You made sure they know that when the time is right and when the

**money** is available, you'll return and show them exactly how you can help their business — and then you can go to your CFO or CXO and figure out terms that work for all parties involved.

## Nothing is impossible; the word itself says 'I'm possible!' – Audrey Hepburn

Building relationships is the key to the sale, and what wins most deals is that people buy from people they like. When you have unique technology and features, or some things are different about your solution but you've got competitors who do what you do, it comes down to what the salesperson brings to the table. It comes down to how you're able to present and differentiate yourself and your company's solution. It comes down to getting the prospect to see you as a trusted advisor so they know that when they sign up, you'll be there for them. You're going to take care of them, and it's going to be okay. They trust you. Million-dollar deals go one way or the other because of that salesperson.

Being blunt can be okay, but it must be qualified by your understanding of the customer's **pain**. You must be confident your value is high enough that price is not going to matter. Your solution may not be the cheapest alternative; in fact, you may be the top-priced alternative. The prospect can get something more affordable, but now that you understand the **pain**, you can bring your value points to bear directly on that **pain** in such a way that the competition can't touch.

Whether your advantage is product feature, support, or future roadmap, your research into the **pain** will set you apart from the competition. It will demonstrate your sincere and genuine concern for the prospect, and it will place the salesperson following this process at a much more intimate level than the person coming in the door right after you.

## Nobody likes to be sold to, but everybody likes to buy. – Earl Taylor

Get in front of these people and confirm the **pain**, confirm the **authority**, and confirm the budget. If **PAM**'s flashing you the green light, you can move forward to close the deal. Between the ICP and the buyer personas, you have an excellent dossier on your prospects. Once you have the map, it's simply a matter of making it happen.

Some big clients want to be wined and dined before discussing details. You run into some of those people (especially at the management level) who haven't been at it that long and want to see a basketball game or hit the golf course. Sometimes, that's part of the million-dollar deal process and a part of being a sales professional.

In some cases, that entertainment piece makes good business sense. To get out on a golf course with an influencer or a decision maker is a fantastic opportunity. You get four or five hours with a prospect, and there's not a much better use of your time when you're talking about seven-figure deals. Just make sure you can discern what would be a waste of time with a particular person so that you can gracefully bow out and find other ways to keep them engaged.

## What you lack in talent can be made up with desire, hustle, and giving 110 percent all the time.
– Don Zimmer

## Should you proceed with a deal if you realize it'll compromise the client company's overall financial situation?

You can't fully know a company's financial situation unless you have access to their bank statements. Your job on the sales side is to know that your deal's either going to save or make the prospect more **money**; in either case, you're not going to be compromising their financial situation. Each transaction is different. The salesperson is a trusted advisor, but it's ultimately up to the client to make the decision. Lay it out for them, and show how they're going to save a significant amount or make a significant amount with your product and get a reasonable investment return. Encourage them to wrap it up so they can start reaping the benefits.

If the deal doesn't move forward, do some forensic research and figure out why it didn't happen. That might take some lunchtime or other off-the-record discussions with the principles to understand what went south. Sometimes, it could be something you couldn't know, such as they thought they had the cash, but then there was a crisis in Malaysia and the budget was reallocated. They're still interested, but they need to shelve it until the next year.

If you realize that the **money** isn't there, make sure to end the interaction so that the prospect is inclined to come back to you when their business is back in growth mode. Always stick with the straight-to-the-point approach. Once you've identified their **pain** and showed them that your solution brings tremendous value, and they say they can't afford it, move on. Do it in a way that they find you to be a helpful and useful resource for them going forward.

You want to leave as much value in industry knowledge and expertise that points to the fact that they'll be much better off with your product or service solution in their shop than they are without it. Make sure they know you will be delighted to come back when the time is right, and when they're in a position to invest in what you do. Walk out the door with everybody smiling and feeling that you are straight-shooting thought leaders and consultants ready to help them in the future when needed.

I suggest that you follow up with them every three or four months to see where they stand. Add value in those check-in calls and meetings with new industry-specific information or trends your prospect will find helpful. People rotate in and out, new CEOs come in, and new opportunities arise. Things can go from the dark of night to a bright, sunny morning in no time for a prospect and instantly you are back in the arena to create value for your client and your company. I've seen it happen time and time again. Keep your iron in the fire, but you must always leave with a smile and full respect. By doing this, you maintain those relationships and those connections to keep the lines of communication open.

## 6. Create a compelling proposal.

Let's say **PAM**'s in the building and everybody is ready to move forward. Everyone agrees that your plan is going to be signed off on to indicate that the return on their investment is there. In most cases, if you have demonstrated that you understand, and are genuinely concerned, and have made it clear that you can solve their **pain**, the price is merely a quote on a piece of paper; the number is what it's going to cost to get to the promised land. The pricing summary or quote doesn't have to be that complex or complicated. It articulates what you're delivering and the investment required to do so. Next comes the agreement, which is an entirely different document that outlines all the terms and legal obligations in detail.

Then it goes over the wall to legal, and that's a process in itself. The agreement could be 15, 20 or 30 pages of indemnifications and termination clauses and service-level agreements. It's a standard part of doing business with major corporations. You've got a legal team, and they've got a legal team. Once the terms have been established around how much it's going to cost, that goes in as an amendment to the 30-page document that both sides review and revise. At this stage, there may be compromises and redlines, so everybody sees what's been changed. Once the document has been signed, you're off to implementation!

## Whenever an individual or a business decides that success has been attained, progress stops.
### – Thomas J. Watson Jr.

If you've done an excellent job, often the proposal will be a simple price quote with a natural close to a sign-off where everybody agrees. You've done a great job identifying the **pain** and how your product is going to eliminate it. The price is reasonable, so — bang! — it's done.

Other times, especially if you're dealing with a public entity or a government entity, you'll have to deal with an extra step. Perhaps you'll get a request for proposal (RFP). You might have been in there for months, working with them on your process and getting it to the point where everybody agrees that this is it, and we're going to move forward. Then, by law, they have to get bids from others for the particular proposition. They issue an RFP (an instruction set or guide that tells whatever solution provider you are how to propose your offering for this specific customer). RFPs can be hundreds of pages long, especially if it's for a federal entity.

If you haven't been in there designing the RFP directly with the agency or with the public company so that it maps out nicely to your particular product offering, you have a low-to-zero percent chance of winning. If that's the case, you have to be matter-of-fact, and decide whether to participate, even though it could be a multimillion-dollar opportunity. Some of those RFP responses can take months of work and tremendous resources to put together. You have to be able to recognize that although the payout is millions of dollars, you weren't there to design the RFP, and somebody else probably has it wired. Sometimes the best decision is to walk away.

**We would rather be ruined than changed.**
**We would rather die in our dread than climb the**
**cross of the moment and let our illusions die.**
– W. H. Auden

If you pursue the RFP, you've got to go hardcore to make it happen. Show your energy and expertise. Your proposal must shine with enthusiasm and passion. Demonstrate a deep understanding of the problem. Show commitment that reflects your organization's genuine desire to win the business and demonstrate what you have done in the past that proves you're worthy for consideration. Make sure it's compliant with the structure they're seeking so that your proposal evaluator can quickly identify each of the sections and how it corresponds to the RFP instructions. The content must be responsive by focusing on how your company will do the work, and not just describe the action. Present the vision of what you're going to do for the prospect in a way that makes them feel they have no other choice for their award; you and your solution fit like hand in glove.

For a presentation for a private company that isn't bothering with the process of a formal request for quotation (RFQ), the best situation is to deliver a price quote and ask for the business on the spot. If you've done your job right, when you get to the point of investment, you have already eliminated the competition. If they're ready to do a deal based on a price quote, your energy, expertise and commitment have already shone through, and fancy proposals aren't necessary.

When the situation requires a detailed response and proposal, it goes without saying that yours must be the most professional in the stack.

Anybody who picks it up and doesn't know you as a vendor should see immediately that you intimately understand the problem, and know how to deliver the solution, and that you've done it before, and have excellent references which speak highly of your solution. After five minutes, the uninitiated could conclude from your proposal that you understand their business and their **pain**, have articulated it accurately, and have shown a reasonable and achievable ROI proposition.

## **A goal is a dream with a deadline.** – Napoleon Hill

Proposal creation requires all hands on deck; everyone needs to contribute. The sales department ultimately must deliver the document, but all departments need to participate in its production. When you look at something like a significant million-dollar proposal, the marketing department must be at the forefront with beautiful artwork, charts, graphs, white papers, relevant analyst briefings, ROI calculators and impeccable proposal design.

The other departments, such as R&D, provide the roadmap. They offer the parts and processes that demonstrate how your solution will be of high value to that particular customer. They provide a view of what's coming down the road and how they might be able to influence new features and delivery timelines once they sign up as one of your brand new customers. The finance department is going to want to know how financially secure you are so your CFO or other finance team member must cast your financial situation in the best light, ensuring prospects see you as a stable, reliable company.

Customer support will provide their hours of operation, service-level agreement conditions, after-hours plans and expectations. All the information from customer support needs to be codified and presented in a friendly, easy to understand format that can be dropped into the proposal. Ultimately, the salesperson is reviewing all the pieces and making sure everything maps to what she has promised to this company. Then she walks in and delivers it, presents it, and closes business. It's a collaborative effort that pays off in spades.

For more formal situations, with an RFP or a competitive bid process, and even in private companies, you must be ready. Have your graphics, product descriptions, roadmaps, financial tools and formal value proposition reviews ready to go. Be light on your feet, move quickly, ask the right questions, and find the **pain**, **authority** and **money**. You want to have all those components of a more complicated presentation already included in your bag of tricks, ready to deploy as necessary

It's much better to be able to pull out the price sheet or the quote and knock it down, but if you're going to need to go deeper, farther and longer, it's critical to have everything ready at a moment's notice. No one size fits all in these cases. When it comes to proposals, that old axiom about life from Forrest Gump's mama applies in many cases — you never do quite know what you're going to get.

# 7. Implementation

Congratulations, you have won the order! Now comes the hard part; you must make sure your solution works. While you may pass it off to your technical team, implementation team or post-sales installers, the salesperson still has to stay in touch and make sure everything's running as it should. You want to have a long-term relationship with your clients to get to the next step in our process and avoid a one-off sale.

There's an adage you may have heard that says you should sell to your client three times. These three stages are crucial in a million-dollar deal, but these broad categories work for just about any significant sale.

- You sell to them before they buy when you sell them on the promise.
- You sell to them after they buy when you sell them on the implementation.
- After they receive the value, you sell them on the understanding that it's your solution that gave them the benefit.

It's after the prospect becomes a customer and is using your solution that the rubber meets the road. That's when a top sales professional ensures they remain on track. Is the customer enjoying the ROI you promised? Are there any areas where you have not delivered on the vision you provided to them when they were a prospect? Will your customer be willing to act as a reliable, ready reference for you going forward?

Your job as a salesperson is to remain the master of the ship throughout this eight-step process as the ultimate relationship touchpoint. If the customer gets nervous — perhaps the project hits a few bumps — you must be there to assure them that their concerns will be addressed. You must have the **authority** within your organization to go to the engineering team or the CFO or the CEO and tell them the customer needs support. Be prepared to act as a client advocate throughout the entire process.

## 8. Growth and renewal

The goal with every sale should be for your customer to buy again and feel comfortable referring you to others. You want to have a great relationship with every customer; the growth and renewal stage is where you get to harvest all the good work and good will you and your teammates have fostered throughout the sales journey. With every sale, you're also planting the seeds for future deals within your existing accounts and with new customers who may be influenced by the positive reference your current customers provide for you.

### The great... is a series of small things that are brought together. – Vincent van Gogh

Ideally, you'll be involved with the client long after the initial sale for relationship maintenance, new product development and future client referrals and recommendations. Your client will need customer support, project implementation and project management at different times, but the salesperson should always act as the overall relationship manager. If your company doesn't offer new revenue-producing add-ons, maintenance or other services, that's not an ideal place to be, particularly if you desire to leverage your hard work in building a rewarding relationship into future earnings.

Maintaining good relations encourages customers to provide referrals and to take calls from your next prospect while discussing your offerings generously. In the best companies, the customer will have access to all the resources they need but if there's an issue long after the sale, the sales rep should be able to push hard to get the customer support people out there right away. No matter what the problem is, it's a team effort to assist the customer, but the salesperson should always lead the charge in the growth and renewal phase. The salesperson is the one who calls to ask, "I need a reference and would appreciate your help." Naturally, you want the customer to have an excellent opinion about you and your company when you're making that call.

### Hope looks forward. Faith knows it has already received and acts accordingly. – Florence Shinn

The benefits of maintaining the client relationship after everything's done and implemented are many. You'll get feedback on your solutions to drive innovation in your own company. Getting credible suggestions for new products is a massive win for maintaining a productive client relationship. Customers become a great source of information on industry trends and events that can affect ongoing and new business for your company. You want to have conversations with them about what they see coming in the next year. What are the big problems? What issues are they faced with that you can use in your approach to the marketplace? The time spent in the growth and renewal phase is time well invested and will pay huge dividends over time.

### Case study: Top 3 tablet manufacturer
### *The Testers*

A large public company that is diversified in eCommerce, cloud computing and consumer devices (just to name a few industries) wanted to become a tablet provider and create a device like an iPad. The trick was to do that at a very low cost (less than $100). They wanted to have something that could provide a similar experience to the one people were having on tablets that cost more than $1,000 (or 10 time their target price).

There was much **pain** for them in building such a thing. One of the keys to keeping the cost down was to ship the tablet with just a bare minimum of on-board storage and allow the customer to buy additional storage for the device separately, via a small storage card that could be purchased online or at a Best Buy, Walmart or any number of brick-and-mortar stores. They designed the tablet with an empty slot for a consumer to buy storage whenever they wanted, which had never been done before. It was an exciting concept and they had very ambitious goals.

The **money** was confirmed as this was going to be a product launch for the holiday season. The prospect needed to get it done, and they were ready to spend the **money** once the solution was proven effective. Their aggressive goals included launching a tablet product line from scratch and zoom existing offerings to become the No.3 provider of tablets in the world (as measured by numbers of units shipped) — and they wanted to do it in less than 12 months. To go from zero to No.3 out of probably 25 to 30 tablet manufacturers was quite aggressive.

The **pain** manifested in how to make this tiny storage card work in all kinds of configurations — with incompatible operating systems and storage file systems — and how to make it work every single time. Our solution did this. We established the **authority** by confirming who the senior VP of Product Management was that had responsibility for the launch. In his charge were dozens of product testers who planned take this tablet with our solution on it, and try to break it with test after test after test, 24 hours a day, seven days a week, in offices all over the world.

How did we win this deal? It was in giving those testers (the real **authority**) robust technology that they could put through the paces. When they found something wrong or identified an issue, we were on hand to fix it immediately. We were on the phone or Skype or email with their teams in China, Europe and the United States. Whenever a problem was encountered, we proved time and again that our responsiveness and technical expertise was far superior to that of the competition.

We built tight relationships with their key evaluators, and gained their trust on a personal and professional level through very long days and nights. These strong relationships combined with reliable technology were the keys to our success. Our competitors had good technology too, but nobody had a team as aggressive as we were in making necessary changes in real time to fit the prospect's needs. After months of these marathon sessions, we ultimately prevailed and won the business.

## Lessons learned

Nothing beats true collaboration in new and difficult technical evaluations. Be available! Being on site is best when the crap hits the fan, as it almost always does; if that's not possible, phone, Skype or other real-time tools should be quickly and efficiently deployed. Take the opportunity to show your expertise and capacity to fix things in real time (or near real time), demonstrating your reliability as a partner. This company has shipped tens of millions of these units now. Of course, the value to us is in the multiple millions of dollars in revenue, but also in the experience of performing under pressure and delivering rock-solid code in record time. This was an excellent deal that's helped us win similar opportunities worldwide.

There are eight critical steps to finding **PAM** and building long-term relationships — and those steps make up what we call **a million-dollar framework**.

Identify the ideal customer profile.

Engage the prospect.

Ask quality questions to establish the **pain**.

Establish the **authority**.

Ensure the **money** is there.

Create a compelling proposal.

Implementation

Growth and renewal

# CHAPTER 3

# THE ROLE OF MARKETING

**Knowing is not enough; we must apply.**
**Wishing is not enough; we must do.**
– Johann Wolfgang von Goethe

Newer companies won't necessarily have the funds for a designated marketing person, let alone a fully-fledged marketing department. Indeed, the 'marketing department' could be you — and you may also be the CEO, accountant and salesperson. Keeping this in mind, I'll describe an ideal marketing scenario with a well-funded corporation with plenty of bandwidth for spend and research, and you can pick and choose functions — regardless of where you and your company are in the growth process.

## Marketing and the sales team must fit like hand in glove.

Why? Down in the trenches, it's teamwork between a well-tuned marketing department that efficiently positions the sales department that win those seven-figure deals. Sales and marketing alignment has never been more important as the buying journey continues. With the right marketing people asking the right questions of the analysts and collecting survey data, they develop the right analytics to identify the right prospects. Armed with the proper information, even a mildly-skilled salesperson increases their chance to get in a prospect's door.

I wouldn't venture to say that the sales department is only as strong as the marketing department in a given company. Why not? In my experience, most of my sales teams have operated with light marketing resources! I've worked with many small startup companies that didn't have excess cash to spend on marketing. What the sales team lacked, however, in multi-leveled information, they made up for in skill and perseverance.

We know that the marketing department's primary goal is to develop the ICP and provide specific metrics that will show the potential **pain** points in the accounts that your particular solution can eliminate. Then they lob these golden nuggets over the wall to the sales department — and all come together to help the sales department close the deal. Let's do this!

First, within the identified prospects, marketing strives to answer critical questions and dial in on the contacts that will be the most receptive to your message.

- Who is experiencing that **pain**?
- What are the possible messaging vehicles they will be receptive to?
- What are the best methods to deliver that message — social media, direct mail, calls, texts, webinars, public relations?

Ideally, marketing is out in the field with an ear to the ground, as well as peering down from the 50,000-foot level in order to identify the dynamics most likely to impact their ICP/prospects. In a perfect world, they are contracted to speak with top industry analysts and haul information in from the field to sharpen their content and approaches. All of this happens before the salesperson engages with the prospect to ensure the most effective use of company sales time is with the most qualified prospects who want, need, and can buy your product.

**Failure will never overtake me if my determination to succeed is strong enough.** – Og Mandino

## Basic materials

The basics include the creation of infographics and data sheets for products and client testimonials. I suggest some of this information be gated content behind a firewall so the only way to get to it is by providing a name and contact information (which will create a warm lead). This type of information can include industry analyst reports that you've paid for or detailed white papers that are more than what you might give away to just any taker.

## Access to data providers

There are many good data providers out there that can be of great assistance once you've identified your ICP. Companies such as DiscoverOrg, InsideView, Lead411, LinkedIn Sales Navigator, Nimble and ZoomInfo are dependable potential data providers for your research and ICP database development activities.

## Website

A website is critical to the success of any firm selling high-value technology or products running from $500,000 to more than $1 million. Your site is where you actively provide rich, compelling content that's easy to access by the people interested in buying your goods, services or products. You need an analytics platform, such as Google Analytics, to monitor your traffic and tell you who your visitors are, how many there are, where they're coming from, how they found you, what they view and where they spend their time on your website. That information will continually help you maximize and optimize the resources on your site, so you will know what to provide.

## Video

Video has become the go-to format for promoting messaging on every medium available, including blogs and all the different social media platforms. Use video as a content component for product reviews, demos, tutorials and testimonials.

## ROI calculators

These are powerful tools intended for industry pros who want to understand how their solution is going to impact their bottom line. The prospect can plug their numbers into your high-level calculator and see real values. This can lead to the next step where they contact you, download a white paper or request a demonstration.

## Paid-for leads

Another component is to pay for leads from sites such as Slashdot, Spiceworks and TechTarget, where your content will be placed in front of their audience. This can include hundreds or thousands or millions of technology enthusiasts, such as tech buyers, recommenders and evaluators. If your product fits in this category, this is a recommended resource for you.

## Webinars

Webinars are critical tools to have, especially for a company without a large marketing budget. It doesn't take much to put a webinar together and throw them up on your site. A webinar with solid content such as a dynamic speaker from the industry, a well-known customer, a demonstration or other compelling information will drive people to interact with you. Doing a Q&A, for example, is much more powerful and less expensive than a trade show. Plus, it can be recorded for repeated viewing. From a budget standpoint, a well-orchestrated webinar is a proven way to drive leads and revenue at a very reasonable price point.

## Trade shows

Consider the shows that best fit your industry and budgets. Trade shows can quickly add up to a huge expense with little return if you're not careful. Trade shows can, however, be strategically utilized, especially as most industries have an annual 'must attend' show or two where not showing up can raise questions as to your viability. Pick and choose carefully where to spend your marketing dollars on trade shows; research and planning are essential when you have a limited marketing budget and resources.

## Marketing automation component

Here you can track what's going on across all of your marketing channels, especially your email platform. There are many products at different price points from the high end to the more affordable end products. Some examples are Burst, Hubspot Marketing, LinkedIn, Marketo, Mixpanel, Salesforce Einstein, Sendak's and TrackMaven. Some companies choose to build custom installations. No matter what you choose, at a minimum, your marketing platform should have scheduled mailings with a funnel/ nurture program that analyzes who opens your emails, when they're opened, what they do and what they should receive next. You could run a different automated process for each prospect depending on their buyer persona. Drip mailing campaigns are also part of the marketing automation component.

## CRM component

From a logistics perspective, the best form for an ICP database to take is in a customer relationship management system, such as Salesforce or Sugar CRM. Dossiers, spreadsheets and other remote databases are also considerations, but these systems become expensive when you start looking at large databases. For instance, if you consider IT managers, directors, VPs and CTOs, there are more than a million of those people in the United States alone! If you develop that database (as we have), it's vital that the data is easy to access and sort so the investment in a CRM tool is worth it.

Segment your database with your top potentials available in your CRM package at the top level for you to work and monitor their progress carefully. The other 100,000 or 300,000 or one million could be on another platform that's much less expensive than your primary CRM system, yet will still allow you to reach out as needed. It's advisable to stay in regular touch with your entire database, because once in a while you'll find that some of those people who aren't in your CRM system will become interested in your solution. Migrate them into the CRM system after they've responded to an email or an outbound campaign, or clicked one of your channel offerings. (Be sure to back up your CRM regularly, and make sure it's available on a cloud service as your ICP database is your lifeblood.)

## It is not necessary to do extraordinary things to get extraordinary results. – Warren Buffett

Let's delve specifically into research, as different types of marketing research are available no matter your budget.

## The Internet is a good place to start — and it's free!

Mid-sized businesses looking to break into the big sales leagues with the least amount of marketing spend must always keep their eye on the primary goal of establishing **PAM** is at the table. Go online to determine at a high level what's going on in your specific industry or market segment. Are acquisitions taking place? What does the activity look like? Which companies are thriving and which are going out of business? Are companies leaving the industry? All of this information can be obtained via Google research and old-fashioned gumshoe work.

## Engage in public relations on social media to build awareness and a solid brand in the industry (and with any associated analysts).

Marketing will create a sustainable lead and demand engine. Duties that fall into this category include management of the website, construction of various webinar series, the development of email outreach and a nurturing track. They develop drip email campaigns for the entire database. These steps are critical for marketing to ensure that the sales team is on target with the right prospects and can jump on warm leads generated by the marketing machine.

The ICP will provide a strong understanding of who your prospect is and what's important to them. Marketing must dive deep to learn who is influencing the ICP — the people prospects watch to gather decision-making criteria, such as industry-specific publications, analysts (and their reports) and industry-known, respected bloggers. Even their competitors are influencing your ICP, so observe them too. Identify who your prospects are watching, following on Facebook, and reading on Twitter. Determine which social media sites they're following, what they do on LinkedIn and what type of conversations they're having.

Once you understand your ICP's social media world, you will be in a much better position to understand the **pain** your ICP may be experiencing along with other issues that affect their business life. When you get your day in the sun in front of them, you must already know who the influencers are, be on their radar, and be able to provide fresh and necessary content. These core pieces are what the marketing department must have their heads and hands around.

## Outside-in analytics are essential for effective marketing as you launch the sales process.

Analytics are all about visibility, and being able to see and understand the market. Outsourcing is a viable tool for this step. It ensures there is no bias on the raw data and will provide the clearest view of the available information, and hopefully lay out the most impactful subsequent steps. At the highest level, these analytics will illustrate which of your marketing plans are working, where people are spending their time, what they're clicking on, why they're calling in, why they're requesting a demo and which particular marketing component is driving the engagement. You can discern what your customers want, where they experience **pain**, what they are willing to purchase and what their journey looked like as they headed toward spending.

I'm a big believer in marketing analytics. If you have the **money**, you can use analytics to shave any wasted steps and reveal a clear path to your guaranteed customer base. It costs to hire outside firms, but that's the kind of detail you need to be effective in your messaging to the marketplace. When you combine the outside-in data with what your salesperson brings back from the trenches, you will have a clear idea where marketing should focus.

An inside-out company will have product marketing people sit in their cubes and guesstimate what they need to be doing and what the market is seeking. They compile some materials and throw it over the wall to sales who then chase down possible prospects. What an inefficient waste of resources! Trust me, outside-in marketing is the more efficient way to go.

For a company just getting started, designing and utilizing an outside-in survey is a robust way to begin. If you don't have any customers yet, watch the market and your ICP (hopefully your first guess is on target!). The outside-in process is easy to pull together, even on a limited budget. It can be done using your internal resources, and you can turn to reasonably priced outside tools and services such as AWeber, GetResponse and MailChimp.

Ensure the questions you design for your survey are on target to deliver the data that will provide the insights you're seeking so you can analyze and segment the qualitative and quantitative data. Having an outside person without the same biases as the internal people taking a look at this information makes a big difference. You can certainly do it yourself, and then it comes down to having opted-in email address so that you can be in compliance and bypass spam filters, which can be an issue in itself.

There are a few steps in putting together and utilizing an outbound survey.

- Develop the goals for the exercise and identify the insights you want to gain.
- Who are the customers or prospects that you're going to put into the database?
- Build your set of questions.
- Offer an incentive and deploy; the incentive will help ensure your targets complete the survey.
- Once you get that data back, analyze it and segment it on qualitative and quantitative data.
- Look for patterns to help you develop your message to deliver the impact that makes the most sense.

Some incentives I've seen offered have included a Starbucks card for surveys that shouldn't be that time-consuming. It should take the respondents a few minutes to fill out your questions, so a $5 or $10 Starbucks card is ideal. Alternatively, you can offer a grand prize, such as a $500 or $1,000 gift card to a randomly-selected participant, plus a $5 Starbucks card for participating. See what works for your particular industry to ensure the widest array of responses.

The expected return rate varies, depending on whether or not they are your customer base; you can expect a 40 percent to 50 percent return in that case. If, however, it's a cold group where the people don't know your company, even if you're asking good questions that provoke responses and offering a substantial incentive for participating, you could be looking at only a 10 percent return.

**Don't let what you cannot do interfere with what you can do.** – John R. Wooden

Once you've received the results from your survey process, analyze the qualitative, quantitative and unstructured responses to understand trends, opinions and motivations. Pull together the structured, more quantitative data so you can expertly analyze the statistical information. You'll uncover patterns that will guide you in creating focus groups, online polls or even telephone interviews to drill deeper into the provided data. Once you have a good base of information, determine what's most important to prospective buyers and existing customers. Hone your ICP to make it tighter whiles sharpening your messages directed at the buyer personas within those accounts.

## If your budget can accommodate the spending, consider analysts with paid subscriptions.

Companies such as Aberdeen Research, Forrester, 451 Research, Gartner and International Data Corporation get into heavy detail around what's going on in the industry for particular companies and industry leaders. These companies do deep-dive research into their verticals of expertise, such as government, financial, healthcare or education.

Naturally, hiring these firms will cost you, but you'll be armed with the latest and greatest data when you engage your ICP prospects in pursuit of those million-dollar opportunities. The ability to translate detailed industry data into actionable information for your ICP will generate credibility and shoot your salesperson straight to that coveted trusted-advisor seat. If you can afford to bring in analysts and data providers, you'll receive a detailed analysis of the industry trends and identify the major players who are exceptionally valuable. If, however, you're a startup without a brand, with few marketing dollars, that's probably not an option yet.

Don't fret. Everybody starts somewhere!

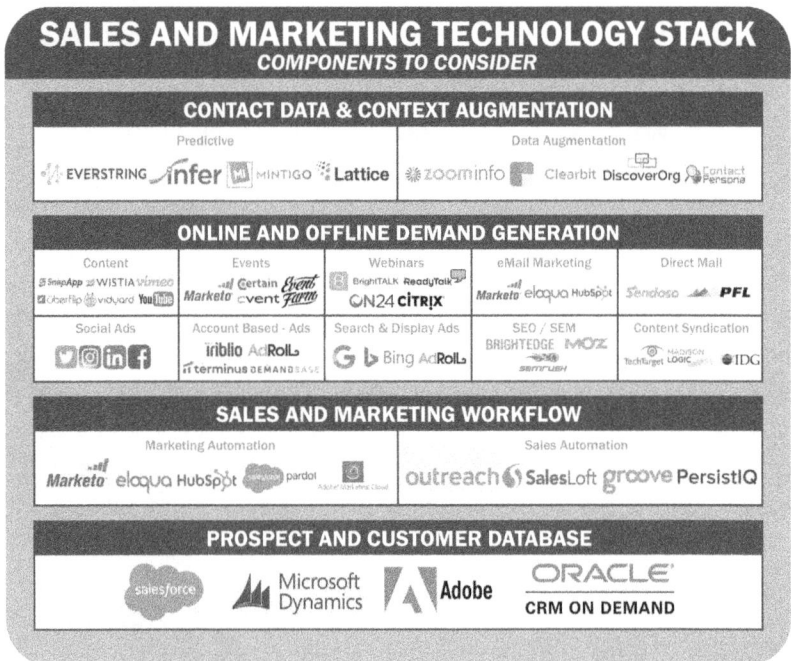

## SALES AND MARKETING TECHNOLOGY STACK
### COMPONENTS TO CONSIDER

#### CONTACT DATA & CONTEXT AUGMENTATION

Predictive | Data Augmentation

EVERSTRING · infer · MINTIGO · Lattice | zoominfo · Clearbit · DiscoverOrg · Contact Persona

#### ONLINE AND OFFLINE DEMAND GENERATION

| Content | Events | Webinars | eMail Marketing | Direct Mail |
|---|---|---|---|---|
| SnapApp · WISTIA · vimeo · Uberflip · vidyard · YouTube | Certain · Marketo · cvent · Farm | BrightTALK · ReadyTalk · ON24 · citrix | Marketo · eloqua · HubSpot | Sendoso · PFL |

| Social Ads | Account Based - Ads | Search & Display Ads | SEO / SEM | Content Syndication |
|---|---|---|---|---|
| | iriblio · AdRolls · terminus · DEMANDBASE | G · Bing · AdRolls | BRIGHTEDGE · MOZ · semrush | MADISON LOGIC · TechTarget · IDG |

#### SALES AND MARKETING WORKFLOW

Marketing Automation | Sales Automation

Marketo · eloqua · HubSpot · pardot · Adobe Marketing Cloud | outreach · SalesLoft · groove · PersistIQ

#### PROSPECT AND CUSTOMER DATABASE

salesforce · Microsoft Dynamics · Adobe · ORACLE CRM ON DEMAND

# We've covered the ideal marketing campaigns and components, but what about the company lacking the cash to implement what I've suggested?

A company can compensate for a weak marketing department by leaning on other vital departments. Generally, the burden is going to fall on your salespeople, and great salespeople can compensate for that weakness. People buying from people is the equalizer for underfunded or poor marketing. A professional sales team with the skills to reach key decision makers and influencers to discover the **pain**, **authority** and **money** in a direct way while delivering all the necessary targeted messages and value propositions is going to win business.

Salespeople can develop the skill set to write emails that get responses so that they get meetings or calls with the people that are experiencing the **pain** and have the **authority** and the **money** to spend on a solution. In other words, they will have to know how to find **PAM** on their own. Those skills will be the difference between a good marketing organization that doesn't have a solid sales team versus weak marketing with a solid sales team. In complex, high-value selling, I would take the latter every time.

## We generate fears while we sit. We overcome them by action. – Henry Link

Solid salespeople are the No.1 compensators for weak marketing, but your customer support team is every bit as necessary. Take the time to show a prospect how responsive your team is in a demonstration or evaluation scenario, and how approachable they are when you're discussing technical issues. It's a huge win for the company to have technical people that can interact in a professional and easy to understand way with nontechnical people.

Your prospect will appreciate seeing your team put on their technical hats and go toe to toe with their own top technical people on the other side of the table. That's a big plus for a company to win in business, even if their marketing department's a few steps behind where they need to be. It's a well-known adage that people buy from people they like — but they have to know you first!

## If you don't give up on something you truly believe in, you will find a way. – Roy T. Bennett

For a lean company that's chasing big prospects, there isn't an ideal number of people you need in your marketing department. It's more about making it happen economically with the most comprehensive marketing program for the least amount of **money**. People are the most expensive line item on your P&L, so I suggest a small, efficient crew to spread your message across the entire spectrum of communication channels (from social media to your website to webinars and advertisements) focus on delivering all those components efficiently as opposed to hiring another body. You must always be looking at the return on investment for every application, and that goes for people too. Do you need that many people? Can you do it with less?

While skilled salespeople often make up for lack of marketing, you must still identify your biggest weakness and train your existing resources to eliminate or mitigate that weakness. If you can afford to hire the talent, look at outsourcing (where it makes sense) to develop a stronger marketing department without spending a whole lot of **money**.

## Is marketing the place to shave when you're looking to save money?

Depending on where you stand with cash flow, take a hard look at your marketing programs under the financial microscope to determine where you stand. How many people are responding to a particular program you're rolling out? How many people will attend the trade show where you might spend 10 thousand or 20 thousand dollars to exhibit? Evaluate carefully where your marketing cash is going. The marketing department can always take a look at their spending, and it can be an excellent place to save **money**. Every part of the company from accounting to customer service has to be evaluated from a financial perspective, and marketing is no exception. Everything that marketing is doing must be assessed for return on investment.

### Trying is winning in the moment. – Dan Waldschmidt

## Outsourcing seems to be the way of the future.

Many marketing programs can be outsourced quite easily. Some organizations are stepping up to focus on doing sales and marketing for particular companies in particular markets and verticals. They've created a scenario where they get a percentage of the transaction or pay for performance. This trend is going to continue, and we'll start seeing smaller and smaller splinters of company activities that can be outsourced. The gig economy is expanding toward this segment.

With business trending this way, it's a great opportunity on both sides of the coin for the vendor with the product and the R&D investment behind it to be able to pay based on performance. It's a great model for the sales team that knows how good they are and understands what it takes for a successful product to be sold. With many applications being increasingly cloud-based these days, you can remotely run much of a corporation.

Beyond the personas and statistics and metrics and content, marketing is ultimately tasked with creating a positive vision of success so the prospect will purchase. Sales then builds on the initial concept and helps the prospect see that vision and grasp how it will eliminate the **pain** they are currently experiencing. Make it easy for the prospect to use your messaging internally to sell your product and service behind the closed doors of their company where no marketing resource or salesperson is permitted.

Your materials, once placed in the hand of your internal champion(s), should be able to close the deal. When you're looking at million-dollar-plus transactions, often committees or specific influencers who could be in multiple divisions and various levels of **authority** are the ones who make the decisions. The vision they have of your business and solution is critical to a positive outcome, especially for that internal champion, so make it an image of success and beauty, one where they can see their **pain** vaporized by your solution.

Write a compelling story of what your prospect can envision when you solve their **pain**. Create a vision that they can buy. Perhaps they're losing millions of dollars due to X, Y and Z, and your product will eliminate that loss. Be clear on how it works, what it takes, and project their return on investment. Make that as simple and straightforward as possible and be able to deliver on it. Your messaging needs to reinforce the vision continually with credible facts and reference materials.

## Case study: Halliburton
### *Oil Rig Tough*

Halliburton is a multinational company celebrating a century in service to the energy industry as one of the largest oilfield service providers in the world. The company has hundreds of subsidiaries with operations in 70 countries around the globe. About 55,000 people were employed there at the time of our engagement. Halliburton needed ruggedized computers and software that could be used in their mobile seismic monitoring system and were easily transportable from oil rig to oil rig in a large aluminum fabricated carrying case.

The idea was to take what used to require a massive tractor-trailer's worth of equipment and shrink it down to fit into a briefcase for easy transport in the rough-and-tumble environment of an operating oil rig platform. Achieving success on this project would eliminate a significant **pain** — the expense of the equipment on that tractor-trailer and the massive crew of personnel required to operate it — and eliminate the time it took to confirm logistics for its deployment. IBM was the incumbent, and with an enormous contract already in place, they naturally had a tremendous presence at Halliburton.

The **authority** was the VP of Field Operations who also confirmed that **money** was budgeted and immediately ready to be spent on the project. A group of technical advisors and evaluators were involved in doing much of the testing of the systems. This is the situation we walked into and **PAM** was definitely in the building (or in this case, on the oil rig).

## So, how did we win this deal?

Navigation of the technical team and the internal politics was crucial. We developed relationships with key technical evaluators and learned what their individual wins were and how to deliver those wins with our product. Whether it was a demonstration of G-shock capabilities, heat and cold resistance or drop tests, we made it happen. We showed them our demonstration systems they could use to rough up, beat up, and test out our offering in their labs, illustrating that our product was far superior to IBM when it came to that environment.

We spent much of our time with the evaluators when demonstrating how our systems worked. We provided complete access to our hardware, as well as to our engineers who built the systems. We showed specifically how our solution would operate in their harsh environment. Lastly, we ensured they were very comfortable with how we had designed the systems to exceed their specifications in the field.

Our bet was with the evaluators — those engineers whose reputations and jobs were on the line with the decision to choose us. We had relationships with the executives where IBM had placed their bet, but it seemed clear the decision would happen with the low to mid-level engineers who owned the project and its results. We, therefore, chose to spend our time with the people with dirty fingers who had to carry our product around. We also used a lot of reference-account selling, such as people at NASA (our product was going up in a space shuttle). We also called in references from some other oil companies that were already using our solutions.

Our process enabled us to make great friends and build relationships with the people who were going to be telling those executives precisely what kind of system they wanted. In the end, we were right, and our friends in the engineering group recommended our solution for a significant win. Our strategy won the day, delivering us a long-term agreement worth several million dollars in new revenue.

## Lessons learned

We leveraged our strengths and references to lock this client in for a long-term win which helped solidify our presence in the energy marketplace — and it was gigantic. Once the deal came down, using the Domino Effect, we were able to move quickly into other major energy providers. Halliburton was so well-known that it made the sales cycle shorter and the deal size even more significant, and that allowed us to grow that section of the business by three times in the next 18 months. This case study illustrates a tremendous win and more proof of the effectiveness of the Domino Effect.

The marketing department's primary goal is to develop the ICP and provide specific metrics that will show the potential **pain** points in the accounts that your particular solution can eliminate.

Resources of a well-armed marketing department:
basic materials
access to data providers
website
video
ROI calculators
paid-for leads
webinars
trade shows
marketing automation component
CRM component

........................................................

# CHAPTER 4

# THE ROLE OF SALES

**The successful warrior is the average man, with laser-like focus.** – Bruce Lee

### →The different types of sales personalities↓

Let's face it — nothing happens in business without somebody making a sale. While every aspect of your business team is critical, it's ultimately your sales team that makes or breaks your business. I've alluded to the Maverick earlier in the book, but now it's time to dive a bit deeper to explain the different types of salespeople. It's important to understand the different sales types and see how the Maverick fits in.

One of the books I recommend reading is *The Challenger Sale* by Matt Dixon and Brett Adamson. It's one of the most widely-read books regarding sales today. The authors describe five seller profiles based on their interviews with more than 6,000 sales reps across 90 companies. They rate them in order of effectiveness as follows.

## 1. The relationship builder

This sales professional focuses on developing strong personal and professional relationships with her prospects. She's generous with her time, and strives to meet every customer need, and she works hard to resolve tensions in the relations.

## 2. The reactive problem solver

According to the authors and their research, these salespeople are highly reliable and detail-oriented. They focus on post-sales follow-up to ensure that any service issues related to the implementation and execution are addressed quickly and thoroughly. If not, they're all over it.

## 3. The hard worker

These salespeople show up early and stay late; they always go the extra mile. They'll make more calls in an hour and conduct more visits in a week than just about anybody else on the team.

## 4. The lone wolf

These salespeople are genuinely self-confident rule breakers and what you might call the cowboys of the sales force. They do things their way or not at all.

## 5. The top performer is called a Challenger.

The Challenger uses a deep understanding of the customer's business to push their thinking and take control of the sales conversation. He's not afraid to share even potentially controversial views, and is assertive with both customers and internally with his bosses.

## Now meet the Maverick.

The Maverick is the best sales performer in the marketplace as this salesperson combines the attributes of the two most successful sales types (according to Dixon and Adamson), namely the lone wolf and the Challenger.

A Maverick is an unorthodox or independent-minded person. She's highly curious, extremely adept when thinking on his feet, and tends to develop exceptionally insightful questions. An unconventional person may seem a bit dangerous when you look at the team structure of most sales organizations, but the most effective and successful salespeople tend to be independent and self-motivated individuals.

The Maverick is a highly engaging, likable individual who knows how to ask the right questions of the prospect in the discovery process to qualify efficiently and to close good profitable business. He's a risk taker, and she tends to act boldly to stand out in the crowd and apart from the competition. The Mavericks will take the **PAM** sales process to the highest levels. They possess superior industry knowledge and communication skills that allow them to reach the coveted trusted advisor status in a short period.

Managing Mavericks is an art in itself that requires the manager to allow enough rope for the Maverick to operate while minimizing distractions, such as administrative tasks and speed bumps. At the same time, the manager must maintain enough discipline to allow effective and accurate forecasts of revenue and expense outlays, and to deal with profitability while not disrupting the rest of the sales team that may require more structure.

## Don't be afraid to give up the good to go for the great. – John D. Rockefeller

Mavericks are different people who can be found through networking, referrals, word of mouth and high-quality recruiters; very rarely through and ads or job boards. Of course, if you use solid recruiters, they can also be a tremendous resource for finding these people, but they will be costly — 18-25 percent of the first-year income as a fee is charged to find one of these highly sought-after salespeople. The small company is an ideal place for a Maverick to contribute his skills. Small companies looking to win significant business need to be bold, and take more risks while attracting this business — and that's the specialty of the Maverick.

Ideally, a company driving million-dollar deals will need at least one Maverick on the team, but be careful. A group of Mavericks would become as unmanageable as a team of running backs! Just like any sports team, a mix of talent is ideal. I would suggest a sales team mix that includes a Maverick, a Challenger, as well as some hard workers and relationship builders to address the different levels of accounts. Established accounts need a salesperson who can regularly visit to cultivate new business and manage and grow (or farm) the account, which would not be the Maverick; a relationship builder or a hard worker might be a better fit.

The Maverick needs the challenge of the chase with a grand cash prize and glory on the back end of a closed deal. He's always looking for the 'whale' to stretch his character and capabilities while maximizing his income. She's not a suitable type to manage existing accounts.

Each type of salesperson can inspire other types. If the manager has done a solid job in selecting the team setting the goals, and placing the fence posts for closing deals, everybody's working to the same agenda. When they get together, it should feel like iron sharpening iron as each type sharpens the others. A good mix of those types of personalities on your team is going to yield the most effective results to cover all sales scenarios.

If you're a small company wanting to attract a Maverick, you'll need something better than just cool technology; you'll need to paint a vision of greatness they can achieve with your team. When you're talking to them about your business, you've got to have some exciting things to discuss, so the technology piece is of course fundamental. It's got to be cool and cutting-edge, and it's got to resonate with them. Beyond that, once the Maverick sees a robust solution he believes he can sell, he's going to want to know what's in it for him from a compensation perspective.

Offer the Mavericks an environment that provides the freedom to close business as they see fit, all while earning enormous amounts of **money** for outstanding performance. Having a compensation plan that's known in the sales community to be highly lucrative will make it clear to the Mavericks that they can earn a significantly above-average income on your team. Of course, if you already have a salesperson knocking it out of the park and making a lot of **money**, that's helpful when looking to bring on another one!

**I must not fear. Fear is the mind-killer. Fear is the little death that brings total obliteration. I will face my fear. I will permit it to pass over me and through me. And when it has gone past I will turn the inner eye to see its path. Where the fear has gone there will be nothing. Only I will remain.** – Frank Herbert

Recruiting Mavericks depends on your budget. The fastest way, if you don't already have specific Mavericks in mind, is to hire a recruiter. You'll lay out some cash — around $25,000 to $40,000 or more — to get one of these people, but with million-dollar deals, they can knock out their quota and will be well worth the spend. If you don't have that kind of **money**, you can turn to your networks. Get in with the right groups in your area, such as the innovation labs, the incubators and the startup and technology communities.

Put the word out through all your channels that you're looking for the top salespeople in the industry. Tell them you're going to be paying half a million to a million dollars a year in commission, and you want to talk to the top players. That kind of talk can help bring Mavericks to the table. Then it's a matter of making sure you get what you are paying for: you don't want to waste six months thinking you've got a real Maverick when instead you have somebody who just wants to collect a base salary for six months until they find another job. That's the art of the sale. You must be able to ascertain what you're buying when you step up to one of these individuals.

## High expectations are the key to everything.
### – Sam Walton

Smaller companies who haven't landed that big sale yet appeal to the Maverick, as that's part of the hunt. Working for a small startup company is a risk a Maverick would understand and enjoy, provided the technology is going to work. They realize taking the risk is why they are paid so well. Once you start selling and having success, you can leverage that into bringing on more of these top-notch salespeople who can harness that initial success into significant revenue for the company.

### →Managing the different sales types↓

Mavericks require a lot of space to win business, and it can be tricky to establish a clear structure with them. Be sure to provide the fence posts and the guidelines to work within as needed for the solution, such as pricing parameters, maintenance rules and custom engineering procedures. The Maverick can't be giving the store away by selling at too low a price point or offering free services just to land a sale. The guidelines and rules that they agree to must be clear when you turn them loose in the marketplace.

You must trust that they're going to stay within the agreed-upon guidelines, then you get out of the way and let them do their job. Allow them ultimate flexibility to make the deals happen, and permit them to work the way they want to work. They must have the freedom that they long for as generally the reasons they've gone into sales is to have the freedom to use their strengths, personality, curiosity and questioning techniques to command their own destiny. Set up the box for them to play in and then let them play the way they see fit.

The Maverick's manager has to be supremely confident in their personality because big egos can become a disaster when working with Mavericks. It's a fine line managers walk; they must be disciplined, but avoid a contest of wills. Don't put yourself in a situation where you try to show the Maverick who's boss. That's a no-win situation.

Managing the other salesperson types is a little bit more hands-on. For example, with a relationship builder, you'll see that she will spend a great deal of time ensuring that the customer's happy. She could spend too much time looking to gain approval from the customer as opposed to pushing to the next sale within the account or moving on from that particular customer to a better opportunity for revenue growth. This is a constant issue with the relationship builder because he's generally not as motivated by **money**. They are to a certain extent, or they wouldn't be in sales, but they are not at the same level as a Maverick or a lone wolf. They require a more structured management style.

The Challenger requires more structure than the Maverick, but tends to be a stable sales personality, a great questioner and a great performer. If you have a Challenger and a Maverick together on your team, you're very fortunate.

Lone wolves can bring in huge deals or crash and burn. You have to have some solid activity guidelines in place that show they're making progress and not silent for a month while providing zero feedback on what's happening in their account base. They have unique personalities by which they can bring in huge business, but they need to be handled with straightforward care. The manager is going to have to get down to brass tacks regularly with the lone wolves to make sure that things are getting done and they're not out looking for their next job.

## Never confuse activity with accomplishment.
– John Wooden

Hard workers can be great, but they can also be distracted with busy work that isn't driving revenue. Hard workers can spend an enormous amount of time making calls that aren't picked up or working on proposals that are never going to be won because they were written for somebody else's product. These type of people must be closely managed as they're active, and it looks like they're working hard, but it isn't clear whether their efforts will result in revenue production.

## The pay structure can differ among these salespeople.

Mavericks are regularly going to make half a million to a million-dollars in annual income. It has to be realistically attainable with a comp plan that you've developed for them. The cash has got to be there. If they're successful in blowing out their quota, make sure they're earning sufficient **money** to justify their time spent with your company. You should also consider some other bling, such as achiever trips to exotic locales, bonuses that are on top of their standard comp plan, tickets to sporting events or the leasing of an exotic car for a year — whatever, within reason, can drive the behavior you are looking for.

There are not separate comp plans for the other types of salespeople. Part of the deal is that a salesperson gets a comp plan based on her experience and her quota and her territory, but the manager must do an excellent job of making sure everybody has enough meat on the bone to make **money**. The incentive is that if you blow out quota, which may be a $1.5 million annual sales goal, for example, then the Maverick is looking to close $3 million or $4 million in software or technology to maximize income. Opportunities to blow out their quota by two, three or four times is what Mavericks are seeking. They want and look for something above and beyond what they're going to find at other companies.

# The role of the salesperson in exploring pain

**Pain** is the big P of our **PAM** triangle, and the first role of the salesperson is to identify, validate, confirm, and then reconfirm that **pain**. To understand your prospect's **pain** and explore how your product or service helps alleviate it, ask the right questions around the REP (revenue - expenses = profit).

Salespeople should be following the 80/20 rule, listening 80 percent of the time. If you're talking, you're not selling. It's your job to understand the prospect's situation clearly, and that comes from asking the right questions and listening carefully to what is and isn't being said. Only then can you determine whether or not this prospect has the necessary **pain** to meet your specific equation in **pain**, **authority** and **money**.

- How is your revenue stream being negatively impacted? What's costing you **money**?
- What initiatives are currently in place to help increase your profit?
- What are your biggest challenges in growing your business?
- What's keeping you or your boss up at night?
- What are the key issues, industry trends and problems that you're dealing with?
- Where are you wasting your time?
- Are there any processes or activities that need to be changed or improved right now?
- Are there any specific issues senior management seems to bring up again and again each quarter and each year?
- What are the Top 3 objectives for the company this year?
- What are those objectives intended to achieve?
- What's standing in the way of manifesting those objectives?

Ask questions to develop your understanding of the **pain** problem. Draw out a description of the gap between where the prospect is now and where they want to be. Examine it together from every angle. You want to position yourself in a consultative role so that after you gather the information, you'll be in a prime position to create a compelling proposal that will close the gap and move them to where they want to be. Of course, bridging the **pain** gap involves your product or service at a reasonable return on investment that makes sense to all involved in the decision.

With the right information provided by marketing and other company stakeholders, the salesperson can be an effective sniper, expertly picking the right target and hitting it at the right time to close a deal, provided the **pain** is identified. If the prospect doesn't have the **pain**, respectfully move on after creating a primary relationship you can regenerate when the timing changes. Place them on a nurture track so that the marketing team can stay in touch through your email platform and other soft-touch marketing channels. Keep them informed about your product line and what you're doing, and share any industry issues you discover that could impact them.

Asking quality questions demonstrates that you have done your homework and are ready to listen to the prospect. It's critical that the prospect feels heard, and that their particular problem is the most crucial problem on the planet to you. Your job is to help them eliminate the **pain** of that problem. Bring to the table an understanding that you see their problem from many perspectives that the prospect doesn't have access to. You already know many different clients are dealing with the very same problem your current prospect is wrestling with, so you can help them as a resource, and be an advocate to get them where they need to be, and that is being **pain**-free.

## Lean in, speak out, have a voice in your organization, and never use the word 'sorry'. – Trish Bertuzzi

I'm going to repeat myself (because it's essential), but at the highest level, **PAM** and REP (revenue - expense = profit) will be the same in every single account. How you get there could vary, depending on the particulars of that account. Which vertical are they in? Are they in the healthcare space or the financial sector? Are they a government or educational account? Each of these markets is going to have different pressures, regulations and industry trends that affect them. As a salesperson, you must have intimate knowledge of this information to be seen as a credible resource.

Once you've identified that they've got a real **pain**, and they recognize that they must get it fixed, develop the questions to define the dimensions of that **pain** and the impact it has across their business both overall and within different departments. There is a whole series of questions you can use to illuminate those pieces of the puzzle.

- How much does the **pain** cost every quarter?
- Is it growing or is it shrinking?
- What approaches, if any, have been used in the past?
- What has and has not worked?
- What other divisions are impacted by this particular **pain**?

Draw the picture and color it in so you have a clear image confirmed by the customer or prospect. Establish how much their **pain** has grown and what it costs them. Listen as they present a timeline in which they need to get it fixed. All this information is recorded as the client confirms it. Help them consider revenue minus expenses, and ask how much solving their **pain** is worth to them.

## The role of the salesperson as a trusted advisor

In becoming a trusted and valuable resource, build rapport with the customer so that they see you as somebody they like who will be on their side if and when the ship's ever going down. Your customer needs to know they have somebody on their team who understands their position and can help them get to where they need to be. That's the objective of every salesperson in a significant million-dollar transaction. There is much at stake for all parties involved.

Make it your goal to be seen as a trusted advisor instead of a salesperson as soon as possible. Your first conversation should show the prospect that you are different from the rest. You're not talking about product and features and benefits; you're asking intelligent questions. You cut to the salient issues of that particular prospect's life to help them clearly identify and then eliminate the **pain** they're feeling.

You offer informed opinions and data points around your prospect's daily activities, interests and industry. You synthesize competitive pressures they are feeling with industry events and dynamics, delivering new insights that they haven't encountered elsewhere. Becoming a trusted advisor can depend on the sales cycle and the decision timeline. The sooner, though, you can offer more value and industry expertise than the competition, the better. Get that label and set yourself apart from the rest of the people trying to win deals.

The crucial part is to reach the prospect and be yourself. Whether it's online, in person or through your emails, the trusted advisor persona should ring through at all times. Here are some critical ideas and recommendations.

- Understand what your prospect faces and what negatively impacts their performance.
- Learn their industry inside and out so you know more than they do about the issues.
- Know the government regulations and tax issues faced by your prospect.
- Know the advantages you can provide with your solution.
- Know your prospect's competition and what they're doing.
- Provide information about the competition they don't already know.
- Always look for news on mergers and acquisitions, stock changes, and unusual profit or losses in their verticals.
- Offer insights that demonstrate your understanding of their market space and pressures. That will set you apart!

Offering insights such as those listed above, without even talking about your particular product or service, sets a high bar for the competition, and it's one they will rarely rise to. As a result, the prospect will view you in a different light. They'll see you as more of a resource that they can trust, rather than avoiding you as they do those other sales reps spouting speeds, feeds and product performance metrics.

It helps if you're an industry expert who can go toe to toe with people at the different levels within an account who are dealing with specific industry pressures. Every interaction you have with your prospect should be treated as an opportunity to add value by sharing new information or ideas that can help them meet their goals.

**The most difficult thing is the decision to act, the rest is merely tenacity.** – Amelia Earhart

## The salesperson's role in the proposal

We've touched on developing winning proposals in Chapter 2, so you know that the entire company must step up to deliver the win. The CEO sets the tone by letting everyone know that a well-qualified prospect's proposal is a top priority and everyone needs to help to develop a compelling offer. All hands must be on deck to make that document shine including sales, marketing, customer support, R&D, finance and operations.

While departments within an organization collaborate on the overall shape of the proposal, one person must own the document. The salesperson is the one with the ultimate responsibility to close the business and bring the dollars in the door. Collaboration is critical, but enforceable accountability is crucial as well.

How the team is structured to develop a proposal will naturally be different from organization to organization. Perhaps somebody from the marketing or technical teams acts as the project manager for the proposal and has the broad **authority** to bring in anybody within the organization to create a client-focused, compelling articulation of value. The project manager pulls it together using all hands on deck, while the salesperson ultimately presents it to the buyer.

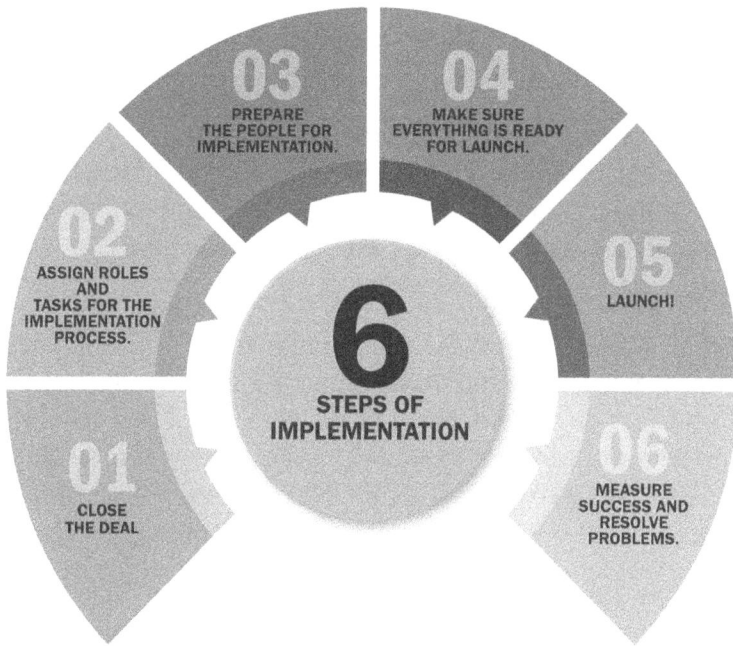

## The salesperson's role in implementation

Implementation or execution is the process of putting your plan into effect. Once you've won the business, and everybody agrees to terms, and the sign-off has happened, congratulations are in order. You've completed Step 1 of implementation. Now it's time to get to work at solving your customer's **pain**.

## The six steps of implementation

1. Close the deal.
2. Assign roles and tasks for the implementation process.
3. Prepare the people for implementation.
4. Make sure everything is ready for launch.
5. Launch!
6. Measure success and resolve problems.

Step 2 includes assigning roles to determine who is ultimately responsible for various tasks involved in implementation. Project managers on each side of the table are named to get their teams in line so the rollout will happen on time and on budget. Responsibilities and project timelines are laid out and agreed upon.

Step 3 addresses the people impacted by this decision; the user community or the people who will use the solution directly. Internally, your client should be getting their users excited about this new solution that will save them time, increase profit, or reduce expense.

For your part, instruct your team to explain carefully how the user wins, while elaborating on the most impactful and meaningful wins for the team. Ensure that the management team who will ultimately be responsible for the success of this system wholeheartedly believes in it. Any naysayers must be addressed and their questions resolved so there are no saboteurs. Once the user community is on board and ready to roll, keep moving with your implementation and training.

At Step 4, ensure that your product or service is ready to implement. Whatever implementation of your particular solution requires, map out the homework and preparation necessary for a successful launch of the system.

## Everyday tasks that happen during Step 4

- Define the processes and workflows.
- Set up new customer fields, categories, time zones and business information.
- Import business data from existing systems as necessary.
- Put together details for any required integrations or engineering work.
- Ensure security is in place.
- Set up the key performance indicators (KPIs) so that you can track the metrics.

Here is also where you begin your training to ensure that the folks who will use the system can hit the ground running. Any particular bugs or pre-production wrinkles should be ironed out here. Your goal is for the first people on the system — your early adopters — to become strong advocates for you to the rest of the company. If yours is a highly technical solution, select the right tech-savvy individuals to ensure early training is successful and that the rumor mill is all positive. Don't shock the end users with too much change, complexity or overwhelming technical jargon.

Step 5 is the launch. Your product has been tested, you've put training in place, and you've optimized it. Now you launch, and get it into production or into use!

Step 6 is when success is measured. Ensure the metrics are being measured, the KPIs tracked, and that the promised return on investment is taking place. If there are any holes in the system or any training issues that come up, address them immediately so that you have only happy users on the network.

There can be significant differences in implementation between hardware offerings and software or service offerings. You can have hiccups in any technical execution. In many cases, you're going to have hiccups with all three — hardware, software and service — at some point. New software could be going on new hardware, along with new services and maintenance offerings. With so much going on, be conscientious and alert. Your team should be ready to jump in, and clean up any messes immediately.

Each area has its challenges. If you're selling a SaaS (software as a service) product and it's in the cloud, everything's already been tested, and it's clean before it goes into a new account. That might be the most straightforward implementation. You turn it on, and it works. When you show up at the loading dock with a bunch of servers and cables to install, as well as new software to be loaded up and then launched, that leaves more potential for issues.

## Fall down seven times and stand up eight. – Proverb

Hopefully, it never happens to you, but if your solution blows up in implementation, you must be prepared to correct any issues as quickly as possible while minimizing loss of confidence or enthusiasm in your user base. If something goes wrong, you've hopefully done an excellent job at Step 3 by setting realistic expectations. When you worked with the end users, you should have provided a clear understanding as to what they should anticipate and why. Your other asset in keeping users on board while you fix any issues is that group of early adopters who should have become strong advocates within the company for your product.

Encourage feedback and make the process for providing it easy so the end user has an opportunity to state comfortably if something doesn't make any sense to them. Any dirty laundry must be aired so that everybody's on the same page in an environment of trust and understanding. Get to those **pain** points before you implement your solution. If, when you are in production, something goes wrong after you've y invested **money** and time and effort in training and testing, that's not good for anybody. That scenario should never happen.

If, however, you find yourself in that scenario, do some forensic investigation to understand where your team dropped the ball, and learn how to improve in the next implementation. To save a botched install and make sure it sticks, you may have to roll out a brand new training program. It might have new features or changes based on feedback. Showing that you're responsive can go a long way toward satisfying the end-user community and getting them back on board with your solution. The goal is to get in front of a situation like this at the beginning of the project by setting clear expectations, making sure everybody's on the same page, and rolling out in a controlled fashion with regular end-user check-ins

Where's the salesperson when something goes wrong in implementation? Right in the thick of it, making sure the deal sticks and refunds don't happen. It's his job to climb on desks, stomp his feet, and get in front of the CEO of his company, if necessary, to keep the system in place with their client. He needs to ferret out any miscommunication or misunderstandings while discovering what happened. The role of the salesperson is to identify the problem and make sure that the system is providing the value the client expected. The salesperson coordinates on the logistics side and works with the customer to make sure they feel heard and their concerns are addressed.

The salesperson is the liaison for the vendor. She is the mouthpiece and advocate for the customer within the company. Perhaps she says, "The end users are not satisfied with the interface. It's much too difficult, and there are way too many steps involved. We're going to have to do some quick updates or changes to the way users input the data, or this deal's going to go south in a hurry."

In this type of scenario, the salesperson has to be intricately involved in problem identification and in coming up with ideas to solve it. Along with all the other implementation people that are involved in a project deployment the salesperson will have the closest relationship with the decision makers. You don't ever want to hear these people say, "This is not what we bought. We want our **money** back."

## You just can't beat the person who never gives up. – Babe Ruth

Hiccups in implementation can happen, and depending on the technology being implemented, they can happen quite often. For example, when your solution involves taking many different data feeds, integrating them, and building many pipes that must seamlessly incorporate your solution into their existing system and network, some hiccups are to be expected. An implementation rarely goes as planned, and a good project manager will mitigate risks up front by doing whatever it takes to ensure a successful launch — which often comes down to ensuring crystal clear communication.

One common hiccup involves trying to go too fast out of the gate. You must take the time up front to be completely organized, and follow a proven process. To minimize issues, proper training and communication are critical elements that must be in place at the beginning of a project. Once a lousy experience hits the rumor mill, it's going to spread quickly, so you've got to be very careful that your first users are happy with your product and remain excited about it.

Once you're at a point where users can start working with the solution, ensure a suitable mechanism is in place to collect their feedback in real time. If a glitch is causing problems in their daily work, you have to act fast to kill any negativity, and get their feedback, and implement a responsive fix into the system. Eliminate the glitch. You want nothing but good, solid feedback from the community that your product is doing what was promised, and that when any issues are found, you respond immediately to fix the problem, and get back to exceeding their expectations.

Carefully selecting early adopters who are technically savvy to receive training and see the value of your offering is critical, as is the useful feedback they can provide at the water cooler. Not setting proper expectations for the community is the most significant potential hiccup in the whole implementation process, so you have to nail this at the earliest step.

The only strategy to address issues is open and transparent communication with the client. Let them know up front to anticipate some issues and when they pop up, explain how you're going to handle those problems. Explain your resolution process so that everybody understands that if something unforeseen happens, you're going to make it right. Have a clear roadmap so everyone on board knows where you're headed and has confidence in you.

### Success is never final. Failure is never fatal. It is courage that counts. – Anonymous

## The salesperson's role in growth and renewal

After a big deal is closed and implemented, it's critical to be in touch with your buyer, your champion and all the people you've worked with so closely when you closed a million-dollar deal. They should hear from you every quarter. Engage them in a check-in call on a regular basis. Ask your new client to be a part of the technical advisory committee or the user group. Find some way to keep them involved with your business and what's coming up so that you can leverage their expertise into new product offerings that they or other potential customers might like to see in an ideal solution.

Keep your customer on the team in whatever way you can. Consider incentivizing them to be a reference account, and keeping them involved in new product offering discussions and industry updates. Invite them to social outings that you know they'd enjoy — a sporting event, lunch or out on the golf course — to get them out of their typical environments, and help solidify your relationship into something long-term that you'll be able to leverage for years to come.

If you discover a change in their industry — perhaps something with one of their competitors — immediately get in touch to let them know you are thinking about them and their business. Maybe you have information about which they're unaware that's going to impact their position in their industry. You want to show up in their inbox with the insightful commentary that shows you're there to help them by providing value. When they go to their next board meeting or budget session, they're going to remember you as one of the critical resources that helps them keep an ear to the ground.

Become an advocate for the business so they call you to learn what you've heard in the marketplace and from the analysts. What are you hearing from the other customers? Where are we going with this government regulation or this acquisition that Amazon made? How is that impacting other people in our industry? Answering questions like these from your clients solidifies your position as not just somebody in the sales role taking their **money**, but as an industry expert who helps them achieve their business goals. The next time a deal comes around, price and margin won't be nearly as important to them. They'll want to do business with you because they know you're looking out for their best interests.

The salesperson's job is to anticipate the client's future needs, and ascertain how the company can fulfill those needs. You want to ease the **pain** that these people feel or will be experiencing by understanding the industry and your particular product category better than anybody else. The salesperson, along with the company's product marketing and management, should constantly be querying what's going on in the industries they serve. Learn the two or three most important initiatives for each client, and ask what's keeping them up at night.

Take all that feedback, along with that of other clients, and synthesize it to form new offerings and products that will inspire them to take ownership of and invest in for faster, more effective achievement of their objectives. In many cases, this feedback is a natural by-product of their participation in your technology advisory board or user group. Those responsible for sales, product marketing and product management must stay in front of the curve, and use that information to fulfill your clients' future needs. This practice is key to enjoying a long-term relationship that delivers value to both parties.

As a best practice, salespeople should always ask clients to provide testimonials or referrals. In some cases, they won't agree to do so, depending on the competitive positioning and what your product does. If it's a competitive advantage for them, or they believe it's in their best interest to let the public think the solution is part of their proprietary offering, they might not want to acknowledge your participation in their product. Regardless, always try to get a public reference on the relationship, such as a press release, to secure their endorsement as a referral for new business. If they won't go public on the relationship, don't worry about it. Continue to provide competitive landscape data and industry expertise that give your clients the insight necessary to their growth and development. This establishes a transformational relationship rather than a transactional one. In fact, always be looking to create a mutually-beneficial, transformational relationship in which you bring more value than cash received. That's the sales professional's job.

## It's not about having the right opportunities. It's about handling the opportunities right.
### – Mark Hunter

It's much easier to keep an existing customer than to find a new one, so it's in this phase that you start looking for ways to expand within the account and increase your footprint. Create opportunities to sell them additional products, or to offer your existing solution to other departments if it makes sense. Spread your wings within that account, deepen your relationships, and leverage your insights to solve their additional **pain**. That's what growth and renewal are all about.

## The salesperson's role in education

A salesperson's day should be analyzed and allocated based on two different time states — selling hours (when you can realistically reach customers) and non-selling hours (when you perform various administrative tasks, and process paperwork). I recommend that 20 to 30 percent of salespeople's non-selling time be spent on the education necessary to keep their saws sharpened.

Salespeople must see themselves as the chief executives of their own business. They're just outsourcing their product development, administration, marketing and finance. Regardless of the company you're working for, you must invest in yourself first by continually seeking ways to develop your skill set, and improve your craft. Make training a continual effort. There's a whole world of training options out there to keep you sharp.

I encourage you to get out and do a training program once or twice a year. Depending on where you want to spend your time, you can choose between business-to-business, inside sales training, driving to the close, impact sales training, strategic social selling for use in social media, prospecting and advanced questioning techniques, for example. They cost **money**, so you'll have to decide how much you want to make this year and how much you want to improve your approach. Remember that the only way that you can stay up on the latest sales strategies and techniques is to be continually working on your methodology.

## If you're offered a seat on a rocket ship, don't ask what seat! Just get on. – Sheryl Sandberg

While some people attend training in person for a few days, there's plenty of online follow-up and training and resources available as a part of different programs. It's a good idea once or twice a year to get into a classroom setting where you're dealing with people who aren't your colleagues or part of your day-to-day career life. They'll put you in the hot seat, ask you hard questions, and make you better at your craft. I highly recommend that experience whenever you can get it on the calendar.

A less expensive way to push your mind and stay current in your methodology is to invest in books such as this one. A fine-tuned text with vital information can open the way for you to new tactics and improved techniques. They can shape your thinking into fresh avenues. I recommend *Consultative Selling* by Mack Hanan, *Competing on Value* by Mack Hanan and Peter Karp, *The Challenger Sale* by Matthew Dixon and

Brent Adamson, *The New Strategic Selling* by Robert B. Miller, Stephen E. Heiman and Tad Tuleja, as well as Napoleon Hill's *Think and Grow Rich*. Each of these classics is a valuable addition to the library of those salespeople who are committed to being the best they can be.

Other ideas, beyond spending **money** to attend boot camps and build your library, include doing some role-playing with other reps or management. Create situations where you're across the desk and talking about real-life questions so you improve your ability to think on your feet. Getting practice in facing and overcoming objections in this manner could give you the boost you both need to level up your sales interactions.

Using a combination of training scenarios is ideal. Read books that take you through specific situations to build your bag of tricks and plan your techniques. Engage in classroom training in which you watch other people, discuss what worked and what didn't, and participate in role-playing to learn how to handle deftly various situations that will come up in your sales career. Practice role-playing with your colleagues in between to keep you nimble.

### We herd sheep, we drive cattle, we lead people. Lead me, follow me, or get out of my way.
– George S. Patton

You should also find a mentor — somebody who has been in your industry for a long time. Let them know you admire what they've accomplished and would appreciate the chance to learn from them. For newer salespeople who have the instinct but not the experience, mentoring is essentially a requirement to pick up the language and nuances of a particular industry. Shadowing an experienced and successful rep is also a terrific way to shorten the learning curve. Shadowing is merely following a colleague on their daily activities for a while to see how things are done. For new people coming on, and even for experienced reps moving into a new company or a new product line, shadowing somebody successful is undeniably beneficial for driving sales tactics home. It is especially vital for junior reps. They should be assigned to a senior rep right away.

As part of continuing education, there are several ways a salesperson can stay up on all the latest relevant details, innovations and strategies in the industry. Join industry trade associations and groups to stay in the know. You'll gain insights into relevant topics in each of the monthly or quarterly meetings. Subscribe to all the important news feeds in your industry to get pertinent reports, and stay on top of the latest information coming into the marketplace. Make time to read press releases for customers, prospects, and their competitors, as well as yours. What's being talked about? What is the press writing about? What companies are making noise? What are your competitors saying in the industry press?

Go to industry-specific trade shows and conferences, and pay attention to where the speakers are focused. What are the themes in the booths? Where are people spending their time? Attend social events and do some online social networking. Follow the luminaries in your particular industry to hear what they're saying. Try to interact, and get on their radar as somebody interested in the space. With persistence, you can build some relationships online with the industry experts, creating more value for your career and your clients.

## Case Study: Comcast Mobile (now Xfinity) *Dominoes — Let's Do This*

Comcast is a telecommunications conglomerate with headquarters in Pennsylvania. Offering a complete range of entertainment and connectivity services, the company is a high-ranking triple threat. Comcast is the second-largest broadcasting company in the United States, the largest home Internet service provider and the third-largest home telephone service provider. Xfinity is one of Comcast's brands, and is used to market their consumer services in cable television, wireless services and more.

The company's **pain** manifested as a growing number of cloned phones that were accessing their network illegally and racking up expensive airtime with no one paying for it. They needed a system to find these fraudulent users quickly and shut them down.

Comcast's technical team had been building some of their own tools to address the **pain,** but understood that their timeline for completion was becoming an issue for management. Working collaboratively, we were able to show them how they could customize our system to incorporate several of their own ideas into our platform. This process helped eliminate the potential 'not invented here' syndrome that can often stall or derail software deals.

The **authority** to make a decision on the deal fell to the CFO and their revenue assurance officer — along with the technical evaluators we collaborated with, who would be working with our products and making a recommendation. Our success was assured by aligning closely with these key technical team members, delivering on their vision using our platform while providing the ROI that met the needs of the CFO.

We had the **money** confirmed through the revenue assurance officer that the budget was earmarked and ready to be spent mitigating and hopefully eliminating the revenue hit those fraudulent users were causing, not to mention the customer support issues the illegal phones were directly responsible for causing.

## Lessons learned

Flexibility and customization can be critical assets at this sales level. We secured our victory by working closely with their technical team to prove our solution was flexible enough to include their in-house ideas. Even better, Comcast was our multimillion-dollar domino in the wireless space, allowing us to move quickly to dominate the fraud-detection market for years to come.

## The different types of salesperson

relationship builder
reactive problem solver
hard worker
lone wolf
challenger
maverick

## The different roles of the salesperson

exploring **pain**
trusted advisor
proposal
implementation
growth and renewal
education

# CHAPTER 5

# THE DOMINO EFFECT

**Do you want to know who you are? Don't ask. Act!
Action will delineate and define you.**
– Thomas Jefferson

Are you ready to knock down all the major players in your market, turning them all into customers with one key win? Let's talk about the Domino Effect.

Researching any market, you'll notice that smaller competing companies tend to follow industry leaders when making decisions. That means one of your primary tactics in sales should be to close a deal with a key player in your target market. Once your transaction is completed and publicized, you can use that win to prove the credibility of your solution in the market, and look at closing new business from your customer's industry peers.

Approach the top dogs of your ICP, reach decision makers and key influencers, and close a deal. You should especially pursue the top players in your ICP database that show leadership and innovation in the space. When they purchase your solution, that sale becomes a massive advertisement for you with the other players in the industry. That one client has become your first domino, and you've knocked it down!

Zero in on those companies first, and strive to make your product central to their operations. Then widen the field to knock over the other key dominoes. Ideally, those smaller companies will line up to buy from you just as their industry leaders do. The cascade of dominoes has begun, and you'll find it shortens your sales cycle when your customer's competitors know that the top dog has chosen your solution over others.

Pick that first domino carefully. Make sure they have influence and a leadership role in their industry, then do what it takes to bring them across the line as a win and a happy client. Leverage that to their peers and run with it. Once the Domino Effect kicks in, you can take out a whole market in very little time.

## DOMINO EFFECT

1. Find those companies that have influence and a leadership role in their industry.

2. Do what it takes to close the deal and make your product central to their operations.

3. Enjoy cascading wins as smaller companies follow the leader and line up to buy from you.

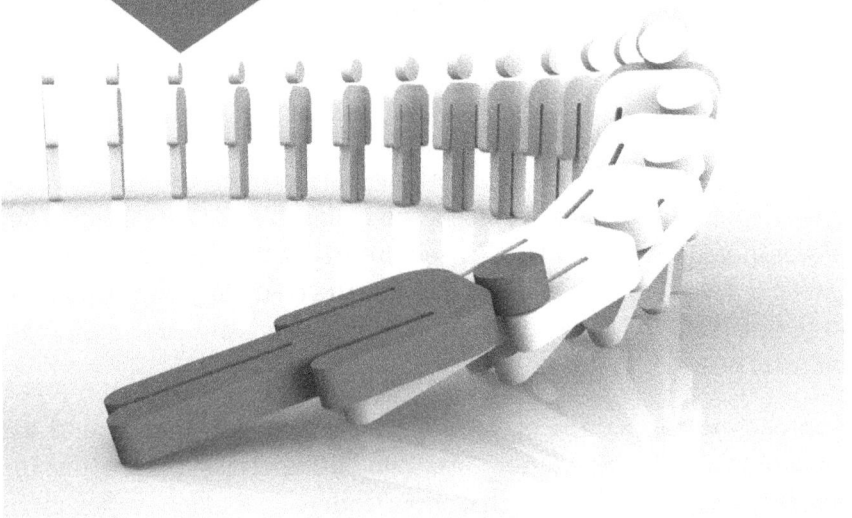

To identify the critical dominoes in your market, define the cream of the crop in your ICP database — the most well-known and respected businesses in your industry. Once you've identified them, it's a simple matter of engaging each of the prospects you identify. That crucial first domino has to love your company, your product and your value proposition in order to become an advocate and reference for you.

For example, consider where particular prospects stand in your specific industry.

- Are they a leader or a follower?
- Are they seen as innovative?
- Are they a visible contributor to the trends in the space?
- Is their CEO or CTO quoted often in the industry rags?

When going after your dominoes, you've got to go big or go home. Go hard after the top dominoes that you recognize as the principal industry influencers and leaders that could use your product. Prioritize the Top 5 domino prospects in your target market and start at the top.

As you strive to jumpstart the Domino Effect, always ask up front if your prospective customer will act as a reference for you. In some cases — especially if it's your first domino — you may create an opportunity for yourself by offering a better deal if they will agree to endorse your product, allow you to do a press release, and use them as a reference. If they can't or won't agree to publicize your deal, make sure the industry hears about your success. Instead of naming the specific company, name a top player in the industry without mentioning their name. Go with whatever you can to make it known to the rest of the dominoes that you're in the market!

When you reach out and present the value proposition of your product, demonstrate through your questions and industry knowledge that you clearly understand the day-to-day issues faced by the prospect — and that you've already solved their competitor's **pain**. Qualify that there is **pain** in the account as you move through the discovery process. Deliver clear statements on how your solution is proven to close the gap between the current **pain** they're experiencing in their environment and the ideal reality that they seek.

Use your key dominoes to demonstrate in a credible way the value in **pain** elimination you provide. Put those reference customers using your product front and center, demonstrating that your product helped eradicate their **pain**.

The domino principle has been critical to our success in the past couple of companies where we have employed this strategy. That first domino deal allowed us to move very quickly into a leadership position and the other folks in the space respected that opinion so much that they signed on very quickly. I've used it several times in my career and highly encourage the use of it by folks looking to dominate their space.

## Case study: Cisco Systems
### *Start with Cisco*

Cisco Systems is a California-based multinational technology conglomerate that develops and manufactures networking hardware, telecommunications equipment and other high-technology products and services. Their specialties lie in areas such as domain security and energy management, and they also offer software services through their many subsidiaries, including Jabber, Jasper, OpenDNS and WebEx.

As they've been around since 1984, it's often said that Cisco pioneered the local area network. When we got in touch with them, we were working with their router group for Wi-Fi. They built a router device, and the consumers buying the routers wanted to attach storage devices to them. This would enable them to have one spot on their network at home to use as a repository for things such as photos, presentations or documents. Their customers desired a centralized storage facility at home. The **pain** was that the router used a Linux operating system and the storage file systems were formatted for Microsoft or Apple operating systems.

What was required was a software 'traffic cop' to sit between the two different environments of the router and storage device and make sure everything worked flawlessly. They wanted the customer to be able to plug in, and it would work with no hassles. At the time, this was a real **pain** that needed a creative technical solution.

The **authority** came down to the VP of product management, the person in charge of the features that were going to be in the router. In addition to the VP was a legion of evaluators and influencers — the people testing the product — as well as procurement which had to sign the order. The **authority** had many faces in this case!

The **money** was confirmed and budgeted as the solution needed to be in place for their latest router line to be successful.

Once the **pain, authority** and **money** were established, we dove in with overwhelming resources to support their intense testing efforts. Their testing scenarios included many different types of storage devices and environments to mimic the incredibly complex potential situations that would be found in the millions of homes where their routers would eventually land.

The plan was to show that our solution was going to work regardless of the type of disk drive platform, file system or environment in use. We made our engineering team available 24/7 to showcase our responsiveness, and show the evaluators precisely what they could expect from us once the deal was done. We tested in all different types of environments; if any issue or problem popped up, it was immediately addressed through our engineering and support team in real time and promptly resolved. We handily proved that we could work in any environment and that they could safely launch their product line.

## Lessons learned

The launch was more successful than anyone anticipated and led to a great relationship that proved to be a domino for us in the router space. All the major vendors came on board as customers in less than 12 months following the Cisco deal. This was a major win that provided a substantial seven-figure payday for our company and solidified our position as the de facto supplier of this type of technology, allowing us to dominate the market for years.

Smaller competing companies tend to follow industry leaders when making decisions; therefore, one of your primary tactics in sales should be to close a deal with a key player in your target market. Once your transaction is completed and publicized, you use that win to prove the credibility of your solution in the market, and look for business from your customer's industry peers. What is desired is a **domino effect**.

To identify the critical **dominoes** in your market, define the cream of the crop in your ICP database — the most well-known and respected businesses in your industry. That crucial first **domino** has to love your company, your product and your value proposition in order to become an advocate and reference for you.

# CHAPTER 6

......................................................

# OTHER INFRASTRUCTURE

**If football taught me anything about business, it is that you win the game one play at a time.**
– Fran Tarkenton

**Aside from your sales team, your company must have the additional infrastructure necessary to support big sales in a business.**

## The role of tech support

In a million-dollar sales-oriented company, tech support is a critical component to landing the larger deals. These types of pre-sales engineers tend to be technical yet comfortable in social situations. Their role in the sale process can be crucial as they can articulate the solutions, features and value of your offering as they relate to the industry issues your prospect is facing. Tech support resources provide some of the most potent credibility to keep a business prospect moving through the **PAM** sales engagement process.

The sales rep can be viewed much differently than a technical pre-sales support resource. Salespeople are paid by a commission in most cases

— and prospects listening to the pitch are undoubtedly aware of this, and that can lead to concerns on their part about whether what is being said is entirely accurate. It's ideal to have a technical resource accompany a salesperson on a call to provide detailed descriptions, demonstrations and specifications. Their presence can help eliminate any sales rep concerns in the prospect's mind. It will educate the prospect and help to draw them to a positive conclusion on what's being presented. For example, I've been in meetings where a salesperson says something, and the prospect looks to the technical engineer for the nod of agreement.

The dynamic is powerful when there's a highly-competent sales support person in the room with buyers or key influencers who are determining which solution they're going to choose. Sometimes, it comes down to how much the prospect trusts your support and technical resources over those of your competitors. The technical support piece is a critical role in any million-dollar type of license or sales opportunity at that level.

People skills are essential. These people must be technical, but also able to communicate critical product details and the value they provide in layman's terms. Many times when courting a prospect, you'll be speaking to a mixed audience that includes highly-technical people as well as operations people who may not have much technical expertise. An influential sales-oriented engineer will be able to address both parties with equal effectiveness.

A world-class, sales-oriented engineering team tends to be full of straight arrows — honest team members who ooze credibility and are also passionate product advocates. They're experts on their solutions, and are familiar with virtually every situation a customer may find themselves in when using the product. One of their top priorities is ensuring a salesperson doesn't oversell what the tech support engineers are going to end up supporting. If the salesperson is in danger of overselling, the engineer can help correct this course of action by having a good dynamic with the salesperson. With regard to the role-playing I discussed earlier, this is one scenario the team should practice beforehand. If the sales rep starts to exaggerate or misrepresent the product in any way, the tech can step in gracefully and say, "What Charlie means to communicate is X, Y and Z."

The worst possible scenario for all involved is to overpromise and underdeliver; the salesperson should never do that, but sometimes it happens. When it does, the tech support engineer must step in and have an honest discussion after the meeting directly with the salesperson. Misrepresenting your solution hurts everybody, and the salesperson is ultimately responsible for the success of that business relationship. They have to keep it real and honest.

## The role of the customer support team

Depending on the cycle of your company — startup, mature, big or small — your customer support's influence will vary. For a more established company with many customers calling the support line, your support team can get a wealth of information from these customer calls. You can learn what's working and what's not, what needs to change in your solution, where it is now and where it should be. The customer support team is an excellent conduit to deliver industry information on the efficacy of different solutions.

I suggest that your customer support team asks callers if they have looked at other solutions. Customer support is in an ideal position with the customer to learn if different approaches are being taken to solving particular problems. A salesperson probably cannot ask and may not receive truthful answers to those kinds of questions as the customer may not be comfortable discussing challenges with a sales rep. A customer support representative is, however, viewed differently from a salesperson and may be able to dig deeper into any problems a client is facing.

When a client or prospect interacts with a salesperson, they might focus first on giving **money** to your company, and then later will recognize the value received. Whereas when dealing with customer support, the customer's primary focus is on receiving value through satisfaction, having their needs and concerns addressed.

Customer support is in a prime seat to gather lots of valuable detail about the **pain** and how your product is working or not. Ideally, you have a process in place to mine the customer support division for their treasure trove of data information. Their interactions with your customer can result in valuable, real-time nuggets of information.

# Case study: Sprint Corporation
## *The Sand Box*

This American telecommunications company is also an Internet service provider. It is the fourth-largest mobile network operator in the United States with a customer base of 54 million. When they were launching their wireless operation, a key component they required for their service was a fraud detection or a fraud assurance solution to be installed. It had to be installed immediately. Without it, they would be losing **money** out the back door to people using illegal phones on their network. Their **pain** was clear to all.

The **authority** was their vice-president of revenue of assurance and security. Sprint had a group of security team members ready to test the system rigorously. They were the real **authority** on the deal. The **money** was confirmed since this had to happen before the launch. In this case, they put out an RFQ, and since several other major wireless operators had purchased our product, we were able to expertly leverage those references right from the beginning for this opportunity.

They didn't, however, care about the reference calls or visits until they saw that we were able to get the system installed in their environment. We showed them what it could do and how it could handle their huge anticipated call detail record volumes. They anticipated growing very rapidly. The system that we developed and delivered to them was highly scalable and was able to handle whatever they threw at it. The decision came down to our team spending a great deal of time with their evaluators, while at the same time being in front of their executive committee with our very professional RFQ response.

The evaluators went through the day-to-day testing on how our product would work. As this was happening, we were exceptionally responsive to their every question, every request and every reasonable desire to modify the user interface for their unique circumstances. We were able to respond much faster than our larger competitors. With our responsiveness, we showed them that our team was going to be with them for the long haul.

The key to winning this client was having our engineering team on site with theirs to make sure that the product worked flawlessly in their environment. The prospect saw that when they needed anything at all, their request was dealt with immediately.

## Lessons learned

We learned to keep our team in front of their evaluation team as much as possible. In this case, they wanted to have a secondary system that they could use as a sandbox, adding an additional license to the contract. Winning this project was a great deal for everyone involved, delivering several million dollars of recurring revenue to our company and a great commission check for the Maverick sales rep. Not only was this a big win for our team, but landing this whale knocked down another key domino in the telecom space.

---

### The role of tech support

They can articulate the solutions, features and value of your offering.

### The role of customer support

Customer support is in a prime seat to gather large amounts of valuable detail about the **pain** and how your product is working or not.

---

· · · · · · · · · · · · · · · · · · · · · · · · · · · · · · · · · · · · · · · · · · · · · · · · · · · · ·

# CHAPTER 7

# MAJOR OBSTACLES

**Wanting something is not enough. You must hunger for it. Your motivation must be absolutely compelling in order to overcome the obstacles that will invariably come your way.** – Les Brown

Let's dive into the major obstacles you're inevitably going to handle as a salesperson in substantial deals. We want to characterize each one, define how it relates to **PAM**, then talk about how a company can overcome these obstacles.

## Seven significant barriers a company could easily face

- fear;
- inertia;
- timing;
- disaster;
- not having **PAM** in the building;
- no-decisionitis;
- lack of urgency.

## Fear as an obstacle

## **Begin by always expecting good things to happen.** – Tom Hopkins

In big deals, fear will often raise its head on both sides of the table. On the prospect side, there's the fear of failure, the prospect becoming afraid during the **PAM** process. They may have had dealings with other sales professionals that didn't work out in the past, such as crossing paths with an unethical salesperson. They may have had a negative buying experience that causes them to feel suspicious or skeptical of your promises. Perhaps they worry that they could be making a horrible and potentially embarrassing mistake.

Fear can easily grip the prospect, so it must be handled early and often in the process by the salesperson through conversation, demonstrations, reference selling and even, in some cases, through contractual guarantees that address particular areas of concern. Together these tactics can overcome the fear of failure on the prospect's side as the fear is uncovered, clarified and handled by the salesperson.

On the salesperson's side, there's the fear of rejection. It's a standard part of the process that must be internally handled by the salesperson. A salesperson must consider his or her personality, and determine how to wrestle with the possibility of failure. Rejection sucks, and of course, nobody wants to be rejected. The fear of rejection can, however, grow into a real monster if it is allowed to fester too long during the sales process. Root it out of you early on so that you can press on and get the deal done. As a salesperson cultivates a relationship, there comes the point in the **PAM** process where the salesperson has to move the deal forward to closure by asking the tough questions that risk potential rejection, disapproval or criticism by the customer.

By avoiding or delaying these conversations, timelines can be unnecessarily extended. I suggest in these situations that you first recognize why the discussion was started in the first place, which was to eliminate the prospect's **pain.** The salesperson knows they can help the customer improve what they do, and can remind them so they can move the transaction to closure. The prospect's going to be a hero, and the salesperson's going to earn a well-earned commission. It's a real win-win all the way around.

If the conversation is allowed to drag on due to the fear of rejection, the deal-making phase can end up being a waste of time for all involved. The salesperson has to eradicate any fear by straight-up asking for the business. In the worst case — if the answer comes back as a no — the salesperson can address why it's a no which is an essential opportunity for the salesperson to expand their knowledge base.

## Some sample questions a salesperson can ask to move the deal forward

- Would you consider a new partner?
- How do you feel about our investment?
- How do you feel about our terms?

Throw these questions out regularly to make sure you're moving the process toward closing the deal.

## Case study: major action camera manufacturer
*Thanks, but no thanks — but wait! We do need it!*

The fear obstacle raised its head with a manufacturer whose main product line is action cameras for mobile apps and video-editing software. They had been dominant in the action camera space for some time, but then the company experienced a tremendous influx of competition in 2015-2016 that severely impacted their business. Their market share was dramatically eroded in the very market they had created as new competitors were coming in from China and other countries with competitive offerings at a lower price point. The company's stock took a dive, and they developed a fear of making bold decisions.

Our product was one of those caught in their fear maelstrom. The prospect could not decide to move forward until we were able to

get in front of the product team and prove how our software —
as a part of their camera — would make a much more compelling
offer and therefore drive more revenue back in their direction. We
were able to break through that barrier of fear to get the initial
meeting, and they agreed to evaluate our software.

We discovered their **pain** was that they needed to bring out new
devices that could support the new Microsoft standard for Micro
SSD cards. This format was called exFAT, and they needed to be
able to use these new cards in their cameras which were based
on Linux, which was incompatible with the Microsoft standard.
They needed the right code and software so a consumer could
plug in their card from Best Buy or Walmart and not have to worry
about things like operating systems or file systems. The card had
to work in the camera without exception.

The **authority** came down to the people designing their new
line of cameras, and that was the VP of product management
and the technical team — along with their negotiation squad on
business development. The director of business development
was a crucial part of building this deal and putting it together.
The **authority** split two ways with the former being the key, and
the latter ultimately pushing it across the line. The **money** was
confirmed because they had a firm launch date for their new
camera line that required this technology. The cash was there.

As their company had been going through some difficult times
with their competitor's offerings getting better and better, this
new line would be integral not only to maintaining control over
their existing market but also to winning new market share. Their
latest offering absolutely had to be successful; failure was not an
option.

We spent years trying to get in to see them, and because of our
demonstrated perseverance, we were finally allowed to present
our solution for their product launch. Our software worked
wonders in all their stress-testing environments, including
freezing chambers and underwater immersion. There were no

problems with our solution, and we were able to build tight relationships with their product management and development teams. These relationships were key; leveraging them helped us close the deal. We are proud to say that the company is now shipping cameras integrated with our software solution.

## Lessons learned

The critical lesson here is never, never, never give up. Even when you've repeatedly been turned away, stick to your guns if you know that your solution will enable the prospect to flourish in new ways, and eliminate **pain**. This doesn't mean you should waste time banging your head against a wall. Use your tools, industry knowledge and references to keep the pressure on to get the meeting at the right level. Work with all their groups and keep showing them a clear vision of their **pain**-free future. After two years, closing this major action camera manufacturer was a great win, getting them over the fear obstacle and signing a high-dollar deal that has opened new markets for their business.

# Inertia as an obstacle

## Motivation will almost always beat mere talent. – Norman Ralph Augustine

Inertia is a tendency to do nothing and to remain unchanged, which is a common sticking point encountered in sales. People generally don't like to change, and many will fight to retain the status quo. Don't fix what's not broken, as they say. Inertia can become a principal impediment to moving the sale forward to closure.

The **pain** may not be enough to create sufficient urgency to propel the prospect to make a decision. An example is when you're trying to replace a competitor in an account. Unless the **pain** is obvious, it's typically going to be an uphill battle to win the deal because the change is a struggle for the customer if they're doing okay with their current supplier.

You don't want to spend much time differentiating your product or service if you run into this issue. If they're happy with their current provider, let them know that with little effort, you're an easy, drop-in replacement, and that your offering will save them **money** and time, eliminate returns, or reduce support calls — whatever your solution is going to do to improve their bottom line. You may have a shot at the replacement as long as it's not going to change their process substantially.

Energetic buyers are driven by **pain**; they wanted to move yesterday, and they're gunning for a change. Inertia prospects who say they're satisfied are, however, a different breed — they live in Inertiaville and speak a different language. You have to show them how your product is similar to what they already have, is **pain**-free to implement, plus they'll get a huge win they're currently not experiencing. The win could be a lower price, free maintenance, free upgrades, whatever your particular solution brings to the table that they're not going to get with the competitor and best of all, it's a drop-in replacement. To overcome inertia, everything has to be easy, and have clear wins for the decision maker.

Do you wonder when a company should decide to go after a competitor's account? The answer is *always*. When you look at most lines of businesses, unless you're representing something brand new, such as flying cars (actually, even in that field there are competitors!), you're going to have competition. If you're selling a payroll system or an accounting system or a backup product, most clients are already using something, so it's a matter of positioning your solution to win their business. Some prospects may be upset with their current vendor for not meeting all of their needs, leaving them motivated, energetic and with unresolved **pain.**

If you call on them, and they say, "We've been with our vendor for 12 years, and while there are a few things we don't like, they get the job done. We're okay and not looking to change." That's inertia. You've got to decide if you can illustrate enough **pain** for them to make the switch to your offering. Illustrating a company's **pain** may require different sales tactics. For example, you might first approach the finance committee with your references to introduce your proposal, and then your introduction to the **authority** will come from the finance people.

# Case study: one of the world's top printer manufacturers
## *Three years isn't that long... really.*

When chasing one of the largest printer manufacturers on the planet, we faced several years of inertia. It came in the form of bureaucracy, as a great many people were involved in the decision to include our solution in their printer offering. Once we got one product team excited, we had to move on to another product team and another and another and another. All the while we had to keep each team continually excited about our offering.

This client is a vast multi-billion-dollar organization with more than 50,000 employees and has a tremendous number of management layers. It was a constant grind to push through the inertia to get in front of every one of the product teams with decision-making **authority** in this particular engagement. It took a long time, but once we were able to penetrate the right levels, we obtained consensus and became the catalyst that brought those different product groups together to agree that our product was right for all their printer lines.

Very well known, this customer ships tens of millions of printers every year from inkjet to laserjet printers and everything in between. As these printers have become increasingly sophisticated, a major **pain** was uncovered. These printers were going to require more storage and the functionality to support multiple formats and file systems. With this new feature, a user with a thumb drive or a little portable disk drive containing documents or pictures could connect their device to a printer, and print from it directly.

The only way to do that is to have some sophisticated, low-level software on the printer that allowed for a storage device to be compatible with the printer, regardless of which file system or operating system was used to create the different documents.

What they needed was a software called Rosetta Stone installed on the printer that ensures all the files move correctly and the consumer doesn't have to worry about the different languages or technologies involved — it just works.

The **authority** was their Senior VP of product management who was looking to take their product lines to the next level. Their evaluators — the people doing the testing — and the procurement team made up the group that would influence the ultimate **authority** with this customer.

The **money** was confirmed once the decision to offer this new feature was cleared by the product management team, and included in their upcoming product line. Our engineering team worked closely with theirs on all the different scenarios where a consumer or business could use their printer. We looked at how they would attach the storage and what potential problems they might encounter, ensuring that our solutions would work through those issues. It simply had to plug in and work — ease of use was the whole idea regardless of platform. Our job was to prove that their ideal could be a reality with our software installed.

We tested, tested, tested, and tested some more — and when we found an issue, we eliminated it immediately, showing the printer team that we were an extension of their development group with the instantaneous response that entailed. When you ship millions of units, there can't be issues in the field. Our quality offering and responsiveness were critical for the company. We were able to convince the product team that our offering was the solution, and we put together a deal that worked for the procurement team's budget and made it happen.

## Lessons learned

Finding **PAM** in the halls of this mammoth prospect led to another seven-figure deal for our company. We made sure we had the right people in front of their people from an engineering standpoint, and built relationships at the senior levels that allowed us to close business in a very complex environment with multiple business units and decision makers — a great deal for them and us.

## Timing as an obstacle

Timing can be a significant obstacle, tripping you up by a change in your prospect's environment. Perhaps you're in the sales process, and **PAM**'s sitting at the table, and things are looking good. Suddenly, though, a management change rearranges the priorities of the people in the deal process — the deal can freeze due to this timing issue. You could be ready to rock when it's suddenly announced that the incumbent's contract has another year or more on it before they're going to make any changes.

Alternatively, the company is bought when you're in the middle of your **PAM** sales process, and all deals are terminated — another timing issue. Perhaps the prospect takes a financial hit that quarter or their budgets are constrained unexpectedly. Sometimes internal politics can blow your deal out till next year when a competing project wins in the boardroom fight for priority. These are all timing issues that the sales rep may not be able to do much about, and any of these events can signal that it's time to fall back and regroup.

Sometimes, however, that timing obstacle may be just a smokescreen, and sales reps must be ready to ask tough questions to see if they can get the deal back on track. Getting to the real crux of the matter could be as easy as asking what else beyond the timing issue is putting the process on hold. Maybe the prospect doesn't like confrontation, and instead of saying the project lost in the boardroom, they ask for more time to evaluate, leaving the salesperson in the dark.

Depending on how strong your relationship is with your prospect, you have to push hard and ask more in-depth questions to learn what's happening. Your job is to get to the truth, and gather the relevant information necessary for moving beyond what may be a smokescreen.

If you confirm that the timing issue cannot be overcome, that's your cue to excuse yourself, and come back later when the time is right.

## Disaster as an obstacle

### You miss 100 percent of the shots you don't take. – Wayne Gretzky

A disaster is an event or fact that has unfortunate consequences, and a sales disaster comes in many forms.

Here are some examples.

- Your product blows up during testing.
- The reference you're counting on says the wrong thing that impacts the overall impression of the offering in a negative way.
- The salesperson doesn't research or build a solid understanding of a prospect before the initial interaction, and gets it all wrong when they're sitting in front of the customer.
- Your internal champion gets fired, leaving you high and dry when it comes to navigating the prospect's internal political landscape.
- The company is sold, and your **PAM** sales process is shut down.

Each disaster has a unique profile that must be addressed by the salesperson in real time. You'll have to make decisions, discover information on the fly, and change course to make the best of the particular disaster you're facing. Disasters are what keep selling at this level exciting and fun. They demand creativity and innovation. These attributes are what keep high-end salespeople compensated at a rate of which most people can only dream.

A disaster generally means that you're dead in the water, and the potential of closing the deal according to your original plan has sunk without a trace. You're going to have to back away, and let the situation clear, then see what pieces of the puzzle remain and who is left standing to help you get the deal back on track.

# Case study: online backup
## *Tough Beta*

This customer is an online backup service provider and one of the most well-recognized brands in the United States. They back up servers and workstations to the cloud. For both Windows and Mac users, documents, emails, music and photos can all be stored in the cloud. This customer has become hugely successful in the business community by backing up entire infrastructures for mid-sized businesses up to large enterprises. They are continuing to grow rapidly, and are now valued at more than a billion dollars as of this printing.

The **pain** this customer needed to eliminate was a gap in their product line that needed to be filled with some world-class software. They needed a bare-metal recovery (BMR). If you lose your computer — perhaps it's destroyed or stolen — and you have to buy a new one, this customer wanted to empower their users to recover not only files but the operating system, applications and device drivers in a simple way. These are all the little things that can be a **pain** to fix when you get a new computer and want your old data and environment placed on top of the new system so you can keep chugging along. When you solve that **pain**, that's BMR!

The **authority** was the CEO and the CFO who would be the signatory, and they would be helped to a decision by a cadre of technical evaluators. When you've got a technical product that's going to be in hundreds of thousands (and in many cases, millions) of end users' hands; you're going to face evaluators who are going to test your product rigorously to make sure that it works in every conceivable environment and configuration. These evaluators can't say yes, but they can certainly say no, so you have to take good care of them.

Of course, the procurement people are involved as well, but due to the importance and expense involved in this transaction, it was the CEO who had the **authority** and direct involvement in making this decision. The **money** was confirmed as this was an essential feature of their new product line to give it strong differentiation in a very competitive space. **PAM** was in the building!

We developed key relationships with their engineers and showed them exactly how the product was going to work within their environment and how easy it was going to be to integrate. Then they hired a new CEO, and he killed our deal by putting it on the back burner. Disaster strikes! We were well on our way to a significant win, then everything ground to a halt while the new team came in and got its feet on the ground.

At first, when the new CEO came in, our internal contacts naturally became a bit about wary about engaging with us until they knew whether they were going to stay the course on our deal. That's when we had to take it up a notch and get the new CEO to see that we were the right people to be working with them on this significant project. Initially he was not very receptive; however, we were allowed to continue working with their engineering team to show them that our approach and what we had done up to that point was of high value.

I spoke with the new CEO and convinced him of our promise and partnership. I assured him that we could do exactly what they needed and asked him to allow us to continue. We proved to him that we were going to be a good partner for the long term and to stay with us. It was a critical conversation. We didn't want him to bring in somebody that he might have worked with before, or be convinced that one of the other vendors in the evaluation along with us might be preferable.

At this point, the relationships we developed with their senior team on the engineering side, along with our superior technology, positively influenced the new CEO and his team. Ultimately, it was the technology we delivered and our access to the senior-level executives in the new regime that won the business for us.

## Lessons learned

Even when you face a potential disaster, if you are genuinely convinced of your value, you have to stay the course and do what it takes to win the business. This billion dollar company is now thriving, and we're right there with them, enjoying the ride and growing along with their customer base. It was crucial to have many advocates within the company who could champion our case to the new team. They knew our capabilities and our expertise and how nicely it mapped to their requirements gave us the edge we needed to keep the deal alive in the midst of what could have been an unmitigated disaster. Due to our perseverance and foresight, we have a multimillion-dollar deal and extensive and deep relationships from the CEO to finance and the engineering team.

# PAM's not in the building.

## If you aren't going all the way, why go at all?
### – Joe Namath

As discussed, **PAM** is the process to make sure that you're spending your time in the right spot, and you've got a prospect who's ready to write a check for your solution. If you can't identify the **pain**, **authority** and **money**, this is an obstacle that you're not going to be able to overcome — there won't be a deal.

If you can't qualify those three aspects and make sure there's an urgency to get the deal done, it's time to move on. The sooner you can do that, the better and more successful you're going to be over the long term. There is *no* time to waste. You must have **PAM** in the building or you're out.

## Case study: major mobile phone manufacturer

No **PAM** = no deal. Unfortunately, we've had a few times when we were unable to find **PAM**. One case includes a fast-growing mobile handset manufacturer out of Florida. They have some great products that they sell on Amazon and enjoy a massive following in Latin America. They have, however, an issue with the amount of storage they can put into these devices because of their architecture's software limitations. We offer a solution that they could integrate into the phones that would allow almost unlimited storage for their devices; a fantastic addition of value they could provide to their customers almost immediately

It's a great use case and an opportunity for a consumer once they have that phone to buy as much storage as they want. **PAM** isn't, however, in the building. At this point, the company does not perceive the lack of storage as a real **pain** that they need to address with their prospect base. They haven't moved forward.

### Lessons learned

Our challenge is to continue to track **PAM** with a minimal amount of resources and time involved via reference accounts, industry insights, competitive threat analysis and other relevant tactics that will help this prospect see the value in our technology for their customers. Eventually, they're going to need a solution like ours, so it's a matter of standing in front of them, proving that the **pain** is real, and driving the urgency. Right now, without **PAM** in the building, we don't have a deal.

## No-decisionitis as an obstacle

Your job as a sales resource is to find and qualify **PAM** before attempting a close. It's imperative that you know **PAM** is in the building and when it's likely that a decision is going to be made. You want to reach the point where you create a verbal contract with the prospect that if you can show them the return on investment, they will agree to move forward. You have to know that your prospect is willing to do the deal with you.

Throughout the sales process, you have to know that you have an opportunity to close the deal. It would help if you felt confident that your prospect is going to get significantly more value than the cash they're laying out, and you're going to get a nice payday and a great new reference. If you're walking the path hand-in-hand, no-decision is not an option unless you've left some rock unturned which should be discovered very early in the process. If you have all the attributes of **PAM** but a decision is not forthcoming, you have encountered no-decisionitis.

## Case study: major cable modem manufacturer

In one case, we had a large manufacturer and service provider that delivers cable services and hardware for homes such as cable boxes and modems. We showed significant value in the performance of their cable modem and routers by eliminating a substantial **pain** for their customer and their senior team. **Authority** confirmed they had the **money** to do a deal; however, they didn't move forward.

This manufacturer had been evaluating our solutions for months with the promise to invest in our proposal based on successful evaluations. We'd tested it in multiple products of theirs and successfully demonstrated how they worked to various business units to no avail. They couldn't decide to move forward and offer the opportunity to their customers — who would enjoy much more capabilities as a result of our solution.

Our job was to track down why they couldn't make a decision and determine who was ultimately going to be the champion to take the deal internally to the next level. The messaging we received was "We're still looking. We're still evaluating. We're not sure what we're going to do."

These are rampant no-decisionitis symptoms, so it was up to us to keep the heat on and figure out who had the most to gain from a more comprehensive solution. We had to determine how long to persist in that scenario, as it was a judgment call that we had to make every quarter.

We wanted to ensure that we were not wasting anyone's time, so it was an ongoing decision-making process. In cases such as with this prospect, there are no set rules because these are big companies and therefore significant opportunities for us.

## Lessons learned

While we didn't want to waste time, we've been through the gamut enough times to know that in some cases, all you can do is wait it out. We continue to show our value to varying combinations of people to make this deal happen. No-decisionitis is a terrible disease that doesn't have a clear remedy. Each case is unique. This one is no different, stay tuned!

## Lack of urgency as an obstacle

### Well done is better than well said. – Benjamin Franklin

In some cases, you can identify where a prospect is losing **money** by not having your product, and their **pain** is proven. You can be speaking with the person in **authority** to make the purchasing decision. You can verify that their finance team has the **money**. You've covered your bases in finding **PAM**, but when you realize the prospect still isn't feeling the urgency to act, you've met the lack of urgency obstacle.

It's a mystery why some prospects just don't feeling the urge to move forward. Forensic investigation can include questions around trying to understand why they wouldn't want to save **money** in the second quarter as opposed to the fourth.

You can ask prospects why they won't move from first base and hope for an honest answer. They may say they have too many other projects going on at the time, which is usually a smokescreen alerting you to the fact that the urgency isn't there. As the salesperson, your task is to do everything you can to create that urgency for the prospect. If you sense that it's not going to happen, move on to greener pastures, and stay in touch until that urgency is there to close the deal.

You can foster urgency in various ways. For example, if you discover that your prospect is losing **money**, yet they're not ready to pull the trigger, ask to move toward with their finance team or CFO. You may find a more willing audience when you clearly explain your value proposition to them and how they can save **money** with your product and solution. Hopefully, you have a champion in that meeting who can say, "We've tested it. It works. We're ready to go!" Get the finance team across the line to move your project up on the priority list.

Another option is to hit other senior executives with your case studies, case histories or white papers that show them that their competition has implemented your solution. Illustrate how their competition is already enjoying the benefits of your product now — as opposed to waiting.

Target whoever could be affected by your offer. The financial officer will want to save the company **money**. The end users want a product that makes their lives easier. Ferret out these various buyer personas, and approach them using the language they understand and illustrations they need to see in order to respond.

Naturally, there can be internal politics (of which you are unaware) that affect your contact's ability to move within their organization. As you progress into the trusted advisor role with your connection, you can potentially help them get what they need. Offer to make the right calls, and bring in the right people from your company for multilevel selling.

## Case study: major software vendor and one of the most valuable companies in the world
### *We have our own stuff... not.*

This company makes operating systems and provides software offerings that are used by just about every other company on the planet in some shape or form. Over the past decade, they've expanded their reach in all different directions with their operating systems continuing to dominate worldwide. They've now grown to become one of the largest cloud providers, and a leading manufacturer of browser agents, and they offer the de facto office suite software product, as well as a whole cornucopia of other software SKUs for offices of every size.

How did a small company like us win a major, high-value software deal from such a large company with a vast footprint of products, and how did we win over their own solutions?

We started our process by looking for and confirming that **PAM** was in the building. We found they had some measurable **pain** in their retail stores across the country. If your laptop or your desktop PC has a problem and you take it to one of these stores, you'll find their group of skilled engineers is ready and able to help you fix those problems.

The **pain** was that they were using too many different tools to fix problems that were walking in the door across almost 100 different retail outlets. Any time they had to bring in new engineers, they had to train them on all these different types of software products, all with different user interfaces, and it was a significant problem costing them time and **money**. The question was "Why can't we use one product that can address these issues?" They wanted to have a Swiss Army knife ready to fix whatever problem walked in the door. They desired one interface so training issues would be minimized, and every store was working with the same tools.

The **authority** was the VP of retail operations, who was the person that was dealing with these training issues on a daily basis. The **money** was confirmed after a detailed ROI discussion proved that the project would pay for itself quickly.

When we initially discussed working with them, they were confident that their internally developed products were all they needed to help consumers with a broken laptop, a software compatibility issue or a disk drive that needed to be repartitioned correctly. There was, however, a myriad of problems customers were presenting that needed to be fixed, in the store, like Right Now! The timing was off when we first approached them because they felt comfortable that their solutions would be enough to handle the various problems.

We kept talking to them, however, and demonstrating the value we could deliver. Our idea was to provide one product that their technicians could use in all of their retail outlets across the globe to fix just about any problem. We offered one interface and one training that would be easy to navigate, as opposed to needing many different tools and interfaces for the various issues they faced daily. Over time, they came to recognize that having one solution with one interface made the utmost sense, and would pay for itself over a short period of time.

At last, we were able to take our product directly to the VP. We demonstrated that with our one user interface, they could address more than 90 percent of the problems that arose. If their customer's system wasn't booting, they needed a partitioning of a hard disk or a re-imaging of a drive. If they bought a new machine and wanted to put their old disk drive in it, we could help. We confirmed that we could efficiently address all of those tasks with one product, one interface, and one training mechanism that met their requirements.

During the evaluation of our product line, we were able to convince the VP that we would be a great partner and that they would find us easy to work with. The technology spoke for itself, as the evaluators were able to do everything they needed to do quickly and easily with our product. Once that happened, we were able to work closely with their procurement team to negotiate a long-term deal that worked for both companies. Although they build all kinds of backup software and tools, they're using our solution. It provided not only a substantial monetary win for us, but also a fantastic demonstration of the credibility of our approach and technology in the market.

## Lessons learned

We were confident that our tool would be easy to learn and their training time would shorten, therefore providing a great value to the client. We had to keep at it until all the pieces fell into place. Our faith in our solution gave us the perseverance to keep at it efficiently until our time came. We kept showing up until there was the right set of circumstances and the right people were there to see the value we were bringing to the table fell into place. Fortune favors the brave and the persistent.

---

### The seven major obstacles a salesperson faces in pursuit of substantial deals

fear
inertia
timing
disaster
not having **PAM** in the building
no-decisionitis
lack of urgency

---

# CHAPTER 8

# MAJOR MISTAKES

**If you're going through hell, keep going.** –
Anonymous

What are the most common significant mistakes made by companies pursuing million-dollar deals? Company mistakes can include

- suggesting the wrong product for the wrong problem;
- lack of flexibility in delivering the solution;
- forcing customers into a cookie-cutter mold / lack of customization;
- not coming out with new product versions regularly;
- not listening to your customers.

These types of mistakes can illustrate a lack of innovation and attention to the market. Not listening to customers can result in significant errors and poor judgment on behalf of the company. There are also, however, substantial errors that the sales rep would do well to avoid.

## Talking too much

**The way to get started is to quit talking and begin doing.** – Walt Disney

Don't spill your candy in the lobby, and talk too much. We have all met the salesperson who speaks too much and never seems to take a breath to listen to his audience — the prospect. If you're talking, you're not selling. Your goal is to ask your prospect questions to help you identify the **pain**, **authority** and **money**, and move the deal forward.

In any sales interaction, your goal is to listen 80 percent of the time. Instead of discussing features and benefits, and touting your product's speeds and feeds, ask questions of the prospect. If you're asking the right questions, the answers should tell you if **PAM** is in the building, and point to how you can position your company and solution in the most effective light.

## Not asking enough questions or the right questions

### The smart ones ask questions when they don't know. And sometimes when they do. – Malcolm Forbes

When talking to a mid-level manager or director, aim to get in around 13 or 14 questions of substantial quality, as that's where you should be playing ball. Gather information so you can provide a solution and prepare a proposal that will speak to your prospect. They should be doing most of the talking, explaining what and where their **pain** is, and answering your questions about **authority** and **money**.

The quality of your questions should illustrate that you are a force to be reckoned with. I've covered questions in various chapters throughout this book. Refer to them, and make sure that the questions you do ask establish your reputation as a knowledgeable resource. One of your aims should be to move into the trusted advisor role as quickly as possible, so your questions should prove that you have access to quality information and you know exactly what's going on in your prospect's industry.

## Selling by yourself as a rep

### Life shrinks or expands in proportion to one's courage. – Anaïs Nin

It's always better to sell as a team. Bring in a manager, product specialist or a systems engineer to show that you're not a one-person band. You want to prove that you have good people supporting you, and you're willing to bring them out and let them interact with the customer.

Pump up your team by bringing along technical advisors (as discussed in Chapter 6) — for example, they are prime candidates to substantiate your credibility and handle any technical questions your prospect may have. If you're moving into multilevel selling territory, bring along whoever is an appropriate match for the prospect's team. Your CEO, CFO or technical director may need to step in and join you for the appropriate sales meetings.

## Ignoring the influencers in the buying process

### Learn the rules like a pro so you can break them like an artist. – Pablo Picasso

If you're focusing on the senior executives by hitting the golf course with them, that's fine. It's a problem, however, if that's your only plan, and you're not spending time with the people who are going to use the product. The technical evaluators are going to be passing along their opinions to the executive team you're wooing on the golf course. Even though they may not be executives, the power of their recommendations undeniably can make or break a deal. Not spending enough time with the key influencers on the technical and user teams is a real mistake in these major deals; the hands-on evaluators and influencers often hold the keys to the kingdom.

When you go after a prospect, you're looking for the C-level executive or vice president who's going to be the decision maker, but many times it's the 23-year-old technical whiz in the back of the room who whispers in that leader's ear on which company to go with and why. Many times, that is how the million-dollar deal decision will be made, so don't ignore the prospect's evaluation team.

## Offering free trials to win business

### Learn from the mistakes of others. You can't live long enough to make them yourself. – Anonymous

Proof of concepts can be a real problem as these tactics can cost the company a lot of time, energy and **money** with no tangible benefit. In many cases, they can go on for far too long. You might lead with a trial, saying, "Let's put this product in place. Try it for six months. We'll get it integrated at no charge and see where it goes." At the end of the trial period, they ask for an extension. They say they need another group to look at it before they can make a purchasing decision. The deal can go on and on! Alternatively, they may not return your calls, or say, "We're done. Thanks for letting us check it out, and we'll get back to you."

You should have, at a minimum, a verbal, up-front contract in which you establish the boundaries of the free trial. For example, you could say, "We're prepared to offer you a free trial, but it will end at six weeks. At that time, we'll have a purchase order ready to go, provided the product does what we say it's going to do for you. Are you in agreement with that plan?" There has to be an agreement in place with a start date and an end date before you begin any trial. I recommend that you don't offer free trials unless you absolutely must, as it can be a significant waste of **money** and resources.

If your prospect is demanding a free trial, and **PAM** is not absolutely screaming for a deal to get done, it may be better to find a new opportunity. Recognize when the timing is not right, and offer to return when your prospect is ready to move forward.

## Not asking for the business

### Whether you think you can or you think you can't, you're right. – Henry Ford

In Chapter 7, we discussed how a sales rep can experience a fear of rejection which they must get past in order to move forward and close the deal. Letting fear rule you and continuing to engage the prospect by reaching out, visiting, and providing industry knowledge without asking directly for the sale is a costly mistake. It sounds like an obvious fix, but in many cases, the key is realizing that the time has come for the direct ask.

Some salespeople, particularly those new in the business, may feel trepidation in moving forward with a prospect. **PAM** is your best friend, and as long as you consistently and thoroughly establish the **pain**, **authority** and **money**, you'll have the tools to bolster your direct ask. If you've done a solid job establishing the **pain**, you'll have the prospect on your side and ready to help you find **authority** and **money** to close the deal.

## Failing to find PAM

If you don't identify **PAM** at an early stage in the sales cycle, you're wasting time. If you haven't identified **PAM** — and sometimes it's not reasonable to expect that you'll get everything figured out in your first sales call or two — that doesn't mean you walk away there and then.

The **authority** might be a little fuzzy, or the budgeting is still coming together but it's not yet complete, but those aren't reasons to walk away immediately. This is when experience goes a long way; it helps you keep your eyes on the prize. Remember that your sole focus is to make sure you and **PAM** are heading in the right direction. Proceeding without **PAM** in sight means you're probably wasting not only your time but that of everyone else involved.

## Being unprepared

### We are kept from our goals, not by obstacles, but by a clearer path to a lesser goal. – Robert Brault

If you haven't done your research and spent some time understanding where the customer is in their environment, you are unprepared. Are they about to get sold? Are they experiencing rapid growth? What if they can't hire enough people, or they're downsizing? Are people walking out with all their stuff in a box? Are their competitors growing or shrinking? Are they seeing growth in their market share and revenue or a decline?

Have your questions ready, and have them answered as far as possible with your own research before the first interaction with your prospect. You need to have a thorough understanding of where the prospect is and be prepared to engage in an informed discussion. Know where you're taking them before you sit down, and establish what you aim to gain from that particular session. Have your goals and game plan in place.

## Failing to pay attention to the competition

Any sales professional in any industry needs to be aware of their competition. Understand what your competition is up to, and be proactive in defending your position with your accounts and prospects. Of course, depending on the situation, if you're displacing someone that's already in the account, you can expect them to come up with a discounted price to counteract your interest. Your competition may lower their prices so they don't lose the account. They may offer new features and functionality or more hours of free service.

Your job is to be prepared for all moves your competition might make, and to be ready to respond with your best offering to displace them. Be ten steps ahead; do your best to anticipate what the competition is going to do and what your response is going to be.

## Not knowing how to overcome objections in the sales process

### I attribute my success to this — I never gave or took an excuse. – Florence Nightingale

Objections are good. Why? Because sales objections indicate an interest in your product, but also that there's a gap between their perception of what they need and your offering. If your prospect is not satisfied, it's up to you to identify the gap, answer the objection, and move the deal forward by filling the gap with your solution and your advisory relationship. Objections should be seen as showing engagement; that the prospect is seeing the potential of your solution as opposed to saying "No" or ignoring you completely.

Do your best to anticipate which objections are likely to arise so you can be prepared to answer them in real time and prove your answers. Understand that the price is never the ultimate objection; it's always a matter of demonstrating the value you're offering far exceeds the price you're asking. Dig a little deeper and be sure they understand that the value you are bringing is being perceived correctly on the other side of the table. Ensure your return on investment is solid as an illustration of how their investment is going to save them a lot more **money** than they will spend.

## Failing to understand that overcoming objections at the level of a high million-dollar deal requires specific strategies

### You can't build a reputation on what you are going to do. – Henry Ford

When objections arise, the first step is to wait a minute; relax and offer a pregnant pause so you can hear what else they're going to say. Understand what they're saying, and confirm that it is an objection; make no assumptions. Try to deduce what's going on in the prospect's mind, and this is where silence can help. Let them sort through their thoughts as opposed to just jumping on their claim that your price is too high — like it's red meat. They will usually keep talking, so you have to be present and listen carefully.

The prospect will sense your energy in the room, so you can't be defensive or negative if they bring up an objection. Lean in and make sure you hear what they say and how it relates to the **pain** you're going to resolve with your solution. The pause is critical; take your time.

The next step is to make sure you have a thorough and comprehensive understanding of the objection. Clarifying questions are essential here because as I mentioned, the price generally isn't the critical objection. Everybody wants a better price, but they'll pay for the value you bring to them. We see that in all kinds of product sales. Why would you buy a Rolex watch when you could get a Timex? It's all about the value perceived by the buyer.

Clarify the objection and ask, "What else?" Keep peeling back the onion on that objection to work out any other issues that are causing the buyer to hesitate. Keep digging, paraphrase their objection, and feed it back to them. Hopefully, you're able to answer it immediately, but if not, you can gain complete agreement and define with the buyer precisely what the challenge or the issue is that you need to solve.

After you've delivered your answer, make sure that they're happy, and that you've answered their objection so you can knock down the next step in your **PAM** process and move the deal across the finish line. If they still have questions or they're not yet satisfied, back up and make sure you've got a fully comprehensive understanding of the objection.

# Case study: major PC and server manufacturer
## *The Orientation Tool*

This major manufacturer of desktop, laptop and server computer systems is based in the U.S., but they're a multinational computer technology company that develops, sells, repairs and supports computers and related products and services. The company sells PCs, servers, storage, network switches, software, TVs and cameras — just about everything that has to do with computer systems and software.

When we started talking to them about multiple opportunities, we identified an acute **pain** they had in an emerging generation of laptops and desktops. These systems would be using modern operating systems and technology, and required a tool that would ensure the storage devices with older technology would be compatible with their new devices. They needed this software tool to be available as soon as they started shipping this next generation of product. Without a tool to orient the old drives with the newer operating systems, they were going to be dead in the water because storage devices wouldn't work with their new line of systems — a big concern and a significant **pain**.

The **authority** was the vice president of product management and a group of evaluators that were going to be testing our alignment tool solution. The **money** was confirmed, as without this type of a software offering they wouldn't be able to launch their advanced and expensive new set of products.

All looked to be on track, and so it came down to us working with their evaluators. We gave them everything they needed to test our solution with all the different types of storage products that they were going to be working with. We placed our engineers on site with theirs to ensure that we had an immediate response to anything that happened outside of the norm so that we could immediately handle any issues or bugs that came up during their marathon testing sessions. Being on site allowed us to make sure that the tool would work as we said it would work.

## Lessons learned

Having such great visibility within their group by having our people on site allowed us to show that our tool worked flawlessly with their new products. They were able to launch on time and create a real success for their company by including our solution with their systems. This win allowed our code to be included on the tens of millions of products that are shipped annually, delivering revenue in the mid-seven-figure range to our bottom line.

---

### The most common major mistakes made by companies when pursuing high-dollar deals

talking too much
not asking enough of the right questions
not selling as a team
ignoring influencers
offering free trials
not asking for business
failing to find **PAM**
lack of preparation
not paying attention to competitors
not knowing how to overcome objections
not having a strategic response to objections

# CHAPTER 9

......................................................................

# KEEPING UP WITH THE COMPETITION

**The competitor to be feared is one who never bothers about you at all, but goes on making his own business better all the time.** – Henry Ford

Why is it important to keep up with the competition? It's not a simple case of knowing what they're doing in the market; they can also drive a great sense of inspiration within your organization. Your competitors can be a great place to research concepts for the future. They can give you insight into new product ideas, and provide new awareness into the industry to combine with what you learned from your customers in your own research. Your competitor can provide a wealth of information, so know who you're up against in the marketplace. Be sufficiently familiar with them so you can determine the best way to differentiate yourself while understanding their products, new offerings and innovations.

When you compile information about your competitors, I recommend that you keep a profile in your company's records. The competitive landscape is a massive part of the marketing side of your business. I suggest that you closely monitor your five main competitors for changes and updates. The data should be collated, and made available to the sales and marketing teams.

Some information you should know about your competition includes answers to these questions.

- What do they have coming out in your market?
- Are they growing or shrinking?
- How do you gauge their position?
- What's their price point?
- When compared, are you priced too high or too low?
- When compared, are you selling the right model?
- Are their offerings subscription-based or a perpetual license?

Understanding who your competitors are and what they're up to can help you better position your solution in the market to win business. How can you gauge how well your competition is doing? Get out in the marketplace and ask questions. Observe everything you can, and talk to people who have used your competitor's product. Ask what they like and dislike about your competition. Gather all the data available from every credible source you can.

## What you can learn from your competitor's customers

Go to the source and gather data directly from your prospects. Ask who else they are considering for this business or who they have used in the past. When you get into a competitive situation where your prospect is using your competitor's product, in many cases they'll be happy to let you know what works and what doesn't. They may be satisfied with one piece, but feel your competition is coming up short in another area.

## What you can learn from your competitor's press releases

How many press releases has your competition released over the past year? What's the coverage about — are they discussing bland product information, or are they highlighting happy customers enthusiastically using their product? Are they releasing more or fewer releases than they have in the past? Who are their most vocal clients? What logos are circulating on their websites?

## What you can learn from your competitor's website and social media sites

Scour their website for news and information about their latest releases. You can use internal resources by asking a team member to mine your competitor's public pages. Have your marketing or technical people do some educated digging. Get all hands on deck and do the spadework; dig for data!

## What you can learn from the analyst community

Asking the analyst community in your particular industry is another great way to find out what your competition is doing. They're responsible for understanding the vendor landscape, so if you're talking to the right analysts in your space, they're going to know your competition very well. They can share where your competition excels, where they fail, what customers are saying, and how their weaknesses can be exploited for your benefit. If you can afford it, having a relationship with an analyst is an excellent use of funds.

## Use your internal resources.

In an ideal world, you have the budget to sign up for a Gartner or IDC membership ($20,000 to $40,000 or more, depending on services), and to get on an analyst call every month to improve your understanding of the marketplace, but many companies can't spend that kind of **money** on research. If you can't afford to hire an analyst, look at the white papers and research documents of the top analysts that are publicly available to drive your research.

Of course, your salespeople are asking a set of competitive information-gathering questions on every sales call to identify and confirm what the competition is up to, what's working and what's not. Never forget to draw on that collective information.

I don't recommend anything like going undercover to get information. I tell people I don't want to learn something that they shouldn't tell me. I do, however, enjoy speaking to the competition so that I can develop a sense of camaraderie along with my understanding of their struggles.

Trying to steal information surreptitiously is going to come back to haunt you, so my advice is to keep it clean.

From time to time, it makes sense to hire somebody from a competitor who can bring a wealth of information to your team, as long as it's not customer lists and or something illegal. It can be risky, depending on their state of residence. They may have signed non-compete agreements or NDAs with their previous employees, but if you can get past the legal problems, these employees can be a goldmine of information.

## Use online research tools.

SpyFu is an excellent resource to research what keywords and ad-words competitors are buying. You can examine their focus with Google Trends, as it will show you what they're using for their keywords. Use your Google Alerts function for all your competitors' names so that whatever they do is going to ping in your inbox. These tools will help you stay ahead of the game.

**A rock pile ceases to be a rock pile the moment a single man contemplates it, bearing within him the image of a cathedral.** – Antoine de Saint-Exupéry

## Case study: Top 2 disk drive manufacturer
### *Should we use it in everything? Yes!*

This major storage technology provider, based in the United States, engages in development, production and distribution of data storage products and electronic data storage solutions. Founded in 1978, for many years they have been building hard disk drives, solid-state drives and hybrid drives. They ship disk drives to consumers and businesses in large volumes (tens of millions are delivered annually). The drives end up in various environments, and the manufacturer cannot predict where a particular drive is going to be utilized.

As their customer base and the number of environments they needed to support grew, their **pain** developed into the necessity of ensuring that their drive would work no matter where it landed. This result was critical to a happy customer base. They needed to have a plug-and-play solution and they had to ensure that customer support phone lines weren't burning up with frustrated end users.

To solve the prospect's **pain**, software was required to be shipped with the disk drive that would act as the catalyst for platform independence. Regardless of whether the drive was put in an Intel machine running a Windows operating system, an Apple product running a Mac operating system or a tablet running a Linux environment, it had to work. Our customer's **pain** was a complex problem that required an elegant solution.

The **authority** to make this critical investment decision to eliminate this **pain** came down to the VP of product management and their technical team which was responsible for rigorous testing that would ensure the technology worked in every conceivable configuration and operating environment.

The **money** was confirmed with procurement as this initiative had top priority and was fully funded. Without a software solution on the disk drive, users would have to find specific software drivers and handle other esoteric issues to ensure everything would work properly. That situation could lead to a support nightmare and massive refunds.

Our technical team worked shoulder to shoulder with theirs to make sure that whatever consumer or business platform they could imagine and test was supported. Our technical team was available 24/7, standing by to handle any glitch or problem that arose. We made sure that everything worked. Ultimately, after intense testing, our software solution was cleared for deployment, and it became the standard across all their lines of drives, shipping tens of millions of drives annually with our software.

## Lessons learned

This deal came down to a sales approach that uncovered the **pain** early in the process. We were then able to set the table to close a deal for more than a million dollars. That deal hinged on repeatable successful demonstrations of our innovative technology and equally innovative engineering and support infrastructure. This manufacturer was very comfortable with our long-term viability as a partner. Another major seven-figure win for the team!

## Case study: major network attached storage manufacturer
*We squeeze to the fourth decimal point.*

This customer is ranked as one of the Top 3 in the world that designs, manufactures and sells data technology products, storage devices, data center systems and cloud storage services. They were dealing with a storage device called a network-attached storage (NAS) box, and they had the same issues as some of our other clients. Wherever these products landed within a business or a consumer, they had to work without fail.

With a NAS box, they needed a software tool that would manage the interactions between the NAS box itself and another storage device attached to it. Understandably, this involved significant **pain** as there are so many different types of attached storage devices they needed to be supported around the world. This **pain** had to be fixed before they could launch their NAS box line worldwide so that it would work regardless of the environment where it was used.

The **authority** was the Senior VP of software services and their product management team. The VP had the power to sign off on the deal, but they relied heavily on the technical feedback of the product management team assigned to evaluate the software. These were the same people who would be supporting our solution once it was out in the field. Naturally, they wanted to make sure that our software would do the job. The **money** was confirmed as new NAS SKUs couldn't ship without this solution included. Otherwise, they would not work in certain environments, and that was unacceptable.

Once again, having our engineering team on site was what won the day. Proving that we could immediately respond to issues that came up, develop bug fixes on the fly, and make sure they were thoroughly tested and ready for production in days — not weeks or months — gave us the win. The customer saw that we could do the job for them and that we were the best partner for the long term. We won the deal!

## Lessons learned

When a customer looks at their purchases down to the fourth decimal point (i.e. a 10,000[th] of a cent), you must clearly show your value in effective ways. Keep your engineers close to theirs, drive immediate resolution to any problems as they arise, and provide an instant response.

The last two case studies personify the Domino Effect that was discussed in Chapter 5. These two companies are well-known competitors, and they respect each other's engineering teams. It's a close industry, and our second prospect already knew that we were working with the first. Once we closed the first deal, the next one happened almost overnight. While you have to be very respectful of non-disclosure agreements and business ethics when working with competitors, companies tend to respect the fact that you are a vendor to their competitor and will undoubtedly move quickly if you can show them the value proposition clearly. These two disk drive manufacturers became dominoes for us in the storage space allowing us to dominate the market quickly.

**There is always room at the top.** – Daniel Webster

Your competitors can be a great place to research concepts for the future. Be sufficiently familiar with them so you can determine the best way to differentiate yourself while understanding their products, new offerings and innovations.

## Information you should know about your rivals

their next offerings in your market
growth / decline in your market
their price point
how your price compares to theirs
how your offering compares to theirs
subscription-based or perpetual license

# CONCLUSION

**I suggest that you become obsessed about the things you want; otherwise, you are going to spend a lifetime being obsessed with making up excuses as to why you didn't get the life you wanted.**
– Grant Cardone

In selling, as we have seen throughout this book, establishing the presence of **PAM** at your prospect's table is essential to making high-value sales.

Why?

Because there is no sale without **pain**, **authority** and **money**.

How do I know?

Crystallizing and codifying the idea of **PAM** about 20 years ago was a career changer for me in every way. The method works.

What's my proof?

**PAM** has been the lynchpin delivering hundreds of millions in revenue to our stakeholders!

There is no way my team and I would have successfully sold more than 200 million software licenses worldwide without the **PAM** sales process.

When you're hunting billion-dollar companies, this is a small prospect base, so the competition to win their business is particularly fierce. This is especially true when you're dealing with high-dollar deals, and you have to stay in front of them and relevant at all times. If a prospect is under contract with your competition, you know they're already spending **money** in your space. You need to prove that you will eliminate any **pain** they are feeling with your drop-in solution to replace the current supplier at a much better value.

Are you up to the task?

You never know what's going to happen in your industry. People move around. Companies sell. An executive could leave the company and take with them the biases that have kept you on the outside looking in. Perhaps the new manager doesn't like your competitor's solution, and is open to trying something new.

The world of sales is always one of relationship building and staying in front of your prospects. They may not have the **pain** if they're happy with their current solution, but part of your job is to maintain contact with them so that if and when the **pain** arrives — you're there with **PAM** by your side.

The **PAM** framework for closing deals is both a science and an art. When closing seven-figure deals, you have to be ready for the inevitable curve balls flying at your face. Be prepared to catch those balls, or hit them out of the park.

You must find **PAM**.

As you may recall, there are eight steps to finding **PAM**, and together they make up the million-dollar framework.

1. Identify the ideal customer profile.
2. Engage the prospect.
3. Ask quality questions to establish the **pain**.
4. Establish the **authority**.
5. Ensure the cash is there.
6. Create a compelling proposal.
7. Implementation
8. Growth and Renewal

No matter what you're selling, it's not about your offering; it's about solving the **pain**. To reiterate our core concept, you must identify and interrogate your prospect's **pain**. It doesn't matter if it's hardware you can touch, software or a service. It's about understanding the customer and asking the right questions to discover their **pain** and then delivering the solution.

You're selling the dream. You're selling the vision of where the customer wants to be. It matters what you can provide to help your customer bridge the gap between where they are and where they want to be. The process is always, however, going to be the same. You identify the **pain**, locate the **authority**, and confirm the **money** is there.

It all comes down to finding **PAM**.

Did you know **PAM** also happens to be a great tool if you're looking for a new sales role in a new company? Consider taking a potential sales role down the **PAM** route, asking these questions.

- What's the **pain** for your potential employer that you can alleviate?
- Who's the person that would hire you (who is the **authority**)?
- Do they have the **money** available to pay you what you're worth?
- Are they growing or shrinking?
- Are they actively looking for your skills?

My last two C-level jobs came from reaching out directly to the **authority** (the CEO or chairman) who had the **pain** that I could eliminate. I negotiated an appropriate compensation package closing for a start date. **PAM** works not only for sealing million-dollar deals but also for landing million-dollar positions.

In closing, I'd like to reiterate that **PAM** is not only an irreplaceable teammate in closing big deals; **PAM** determines how you win or lose the business. **PAM** makes the ultimate decision on every deal — because if she's not in the building, you shouldn't be there either. **PAM** can be elusive, but find her, become familiar with her, and you'll win more business than ever before.

# ACKNOWLEDGEMENTS

## My Creator

Thank You, God, for Your Son Jesus Christ and for the amazing opportunities You have so abundantly provided!

## My wife and family

Next to God, I have to start by thanking Kerry, my beautiful, unselfish, thoughtful and awesome wife. From her advice to pursue this project in the first place to giving her blessing on the cover and keeping me motivated to get it done, I am truly blessed. Thank you so much. You make me want to be a better man every day.

To my boys, Jake, Matt, Mark and Jack — thanks for inspiring me to be the best I can be as a father, friend and sparring partner. You young men are simply unsurpassed winners and I am so excited to see where you decide to spend your time and immeasurable talents in this world!

## My team

Without the experience and support from my team over the past 25 years, this book would not exist. Thank you for letting me serve alongside you and for showing up every day, and helping our customers take care of their businesses with our software and services. I am honored to have worked with such talent. A very heartfelt appreciation to that special group that has been with me over the last decade and more: Cisco, Jim, Grace and Ross. What a ride together so far — and the best is yet to come!

A special thanks to those amazing salespeople that taught me so much and validated the concepts in this book on the street. Your creativity, street smarts, strong relationship skills and closing capabilities are world-class and well worth writing a book about. A sincere shout-out to David Zinke, the first Maverick sales star I had the pleasure to work with; he helped frame the **PAM** principles more than two decades ago.

## My publishing team

Having an idea for a book is one thing; turning it into something you can hold in your hand and actually read is something entirely different! The experience has been exciting, challenging, frustrating and rewarding all at the same time. Huge thanks to my publishing team, Alinka and Deborah, for keeping us on track and moving forward through all kinds of edits and graphic designs — and special thanks to Marlayna who kept me fully engaged and excited to keep pressing onward, even when discouraged and doubting the process. I also had some great help from many friends, in particular those familiar with the publishing procedure, as they provided excellent insights and advice — a big thank you to Jayson Yardley and Ted Larkins; your input was fantastic and appreciated.

## My coaches and mentors

The world is a better place thanks to people who want to develop and lead others. Special thanks to those that helped me so much to grow as an athlete and competitor in my high school and college days: coaches Tom Baack and the late Floyd Theard. My thanks to all those who took me under their wing and taught me how business really works — Dennis Andrews, Jack Finnell, Jess Hartman, Rich Lull, the crew at Vistage, and so many others.

## My high-value customers

Thanks to those special customers that taught me what it takes to win high-dollar deals at the highest levels, including Acer, AirTouch, Amazon, American Airlines, ASUS, Belkin, Bell South, Carbonite, Cisco, Comcast, Dell, Ericsson, GoPro, Halliburton, HP, Iusacell (AT&T Mexico), Lenovo, Malaysia Telecom, Netgear, Nextel, Nvidia, Orange UK, PacBell, Seagate, Sprint, Toshiba, WD and so many others. I thank you!

# RECOMMENDED READING

Allen, James. *As a Man Thinketh*.

Alessandra, Tony. *Non-Manipulative Selling*.

Bettger, Frank. *How I Raised Myself from Failure to Success in Selling*.

The Bible (especially Proverbs).

Brande, Dorothea. *Wake Up and Live!: A Formula for Success that Works*.

Christensen, Clayton M. *The Innovator's Dilemma: When New Technologies Cause Great Firms to Fail*.

Dixon, Matthew, and Brent Adamson. *The Challenger Sale: Taking Control of the Customer Conversation*.

Dooley, Mike. *Infinite Possibilities: The Art of Living Your Dreams*.

Elrod, Hal. *The Miracle Equation: The Two Decisions That Move Your Biggest Goals from Possible, to Probable, to Inevitable*.

Finnell, Jack. *Do You Want to Be a Leader or a Manager?: If You Can Do One, You Can Do Both*.

Frankl, Viktor E. *Man's Search for Meaning*.

Gilbert, Elizabeth. *Big Magic: Creative Living Beyond Fear*.

Hanan, Mack. *Consultative Selling: The Hanan Formula for High-Margin Sales at High Levels*.

Hanan, Mack, and Peter Karp. *Competing on Value*.

Hardy, Benjamin P. *Willpower Doesn't Work: Discover the Hidden Keys to Success*

Hill, Napoleon. *Think and Grow Rich: The Original, an Official Publication of The Napoleon Hill Foundation*.

Jeffers, Susan. *Feel the Fear and Do It Anyway.*

Larkins, Ted. *Get To Be Happy: Stories and Secrets to Loving the Sh\*t Out Of Life.*

McKeown, Greg. *Essentialism: The Disciplined Pursuit of Less.*

Miller, Robert B., et al. *The New Strategic Selling: The Unique Sales System Proven Successful by the World's Best Companies.*

Rackham, Neil. *SPIN Selling.*

Ross, Aaron, and Marylou Tyler. *Predictable Revenue: Turn Your Business Into a Sales Machine with the $100 Million Best Practices of Salesforce.com.*

Schwartz, David J. *The Magic of Thinking Big.*

Tolle, Eckhart. *The Power of Now: A Guide to Spiritual Enlightenment.*

Waitzkin, Josh. *The Art of Learning: An Inner Journey to Optimal Performance.*

Weinberg, Gabriel, and Justin Mares. *Traction: How Any Startup Can Achieve Explosive Customer Growth.*

Wooden, John. *Wooden: A Lifetime of Observations and Reflections On and Off the Court.*

# FREE SUPPLEMENT!

Are you searching for the key to staying healthy and setting yourself up for success?

You need to take your MEDS! I created my own personal system that helps me achieve peak performance on a daily basis and I want to share it with you.

**TAKE YOUR**
# MEDS

*MORNING ROUTINE*
*EXERCISE · DIET · SLEEP*

**TOM FEDRO**

Go to www.tomfedro.com and download your free copy of Take Your MEDS to see how you can apply and benefit from some of the same ideas that have worked so well for me.

www.ingramcontent.com/pod-product-compliance
Lightning Source LLC
Chambersburg PA
CBHW020207200326
41521CB00005BA/271